Stock Investing Made Simple

Your Guided Tour to Getting Started

Weiss Ratings, Inc.
15430 Endeavour Drive
Jupiter, FL 33478

First printing 2004

ISBN 1-58773-257-2

Library of Congress Control Number: 2004112637

ATTENTION LIBRARIES, CORPORATIONS, UNIVERSITIES, COLLEGES, AND PROFESSIONAL ORGANIZATIONS: Quantity discounts are available on bulk purchases of this book for educational, gift purposes, or as premiums for increasing magazine subscriptions or renewals. Special books or book excerpts can also be created to fit specific needs. For information, please contact Weiss Ratings, Inc. at 1-800-289-9222.

Data Source: COMPUSTAT® Data provided by Standard & Poor's, a division of The McGraw-Hill Companies, Inc.

Acknowledgments

Stock Investing Made Simple
is the culmination of work performed
by many individuals. Each played an important
role in bringing this book to you.
Thanks to the entire Weiss Ratings team
for their enthusiasm toward
this exciting project.
Thanks to all those that helped
on brainstorming and getting
this project off the ground.

With Special Thanks to:

Melissa Gannon, Vice President
George Gartner, Senior Programmer
Shelley Klovsky, Director of Sales
Monica Lewman-Garcia,
Product Development Manager
Jennifer Moran, Director of Marketing
Maryellen Murphy, Public Relations Manager
Cindy Nelson, Senior Production Assistant
Donna O'Rourke, Project Coordinator
Dorianne Perrucci, Senior Writer
Christine Stickney, Graphic Designer
Art Waligora, Illustrator
Jessica Wang, Financial Analyst

Contents

Welcome to Stock Investing Made Simple

Your Guided Tour to Getting Started

If you've ever thought about investing in stocks, but didn't know how or where to get started, then this book is for you.

Maybe you picked up this book and joined the tour because the title jumped out at you. Or maybe the librarian pointed us out and suggested you give us a look. Or perhaps you discovered us while browsing through the personal finance section of your local bookstore!

However you found us, we're glad you did, because we mean what we say in the title of this new book. We're hopeful that our new publication will live up to its name and help you, the beginner, get started as a stock investor. .

"Why should I even try?" you ask. The stock market is just too hard for the average person to figure out. Besides, just look at the evening news — the stock market is too dangerous for beginners.

You think that the world of investing is only for the super wealthy? That world of wealth is for you too — and you can learn to share in it! That's why we wrote this book. If you can honestly answer yes to any one of the following questions, then read on:

▲ Are you a beginning investor with little or no money to invest in the market?

▲ Like most Americans, you may already have a toe in the market — without realizing it — through your company's 401(k) plan. But like the vast majority of participants, you could also do more to maximize the investing power of the dollars in your account. How? By investing in the stock market. Have you studied your choices lately? When was the last time you made any changes?

▲ Are you afraid to get into the market after watching family or friends or yourself get tossed aside by a runaway good (bull) market or chased away by the bad (bear) market recently?

Investors lost a shocking 51% on their investments from March 2000, when the bear started to roar, to October 2002, when the bull began charging back onto the scene. But that's no reason to stay on the sidelines indefinitely. You can get into the market confidently by learning to manage risk.

There are a ton of books to read about stock investing and a lot of them are written just for you, the beginner. So why read ours?

Good question! That's the type of question we're going to teach you to use to your advantage when a stranger asks you to give up your hard-earned money and go with them into unfamiliar territory. One of the most dangerous things a person can do is follow the wrong guide into unknown and unpredictable territory. You want your leader to be someone who "knows the territory" and understands where the quicksand, the rocks, and the wild animals are located. You want a guide who's not only survived the jungle a few times, but found his or her way out safely — and even learned a trick or two to pass on!

But ...

If you don't have the right guide, the strange new world of stock investing truly is a scary, and dangerous trip into the unknown for you, the beginning investor. That's why we wrote this book.

Why Weiss?

A companion book to our *Ultimate Guided Tour of Stock Investing,* **Stock Investing Made Simple: Your Guided Tour to Getting Started** is written and designed to take the guesswork and anxiety out of choosing stocks. The text is written in brief chapters so you won't get overloaded with information and give up. Pick this book up and read it whenever you have questions about a specific topic. Come back and visit whenever you're ready to track down more information about stock investing.

You just don't feel comfortable with the world of investing? Well, you've come to the right place for a step-by-step education.

Our team has provided you with a combination of accurate consumer protection analyses and independent investment ratings that will help guide you when evaluating stocks as an investment. Our book explains the essentials of investing in stocks using easy-to-understand language and a safari theme. We think this one-two combination will help make stock investing simple!

We look forward to adding your testimonials and comments to the next edition of this publication. So, call us at **800-289-9222** or send an e-mail to **comments@weissratings.com** to get your name and comment added to the next edition!

If you really want to understand how things work and learn to invest for yourself — then read on!

Hey, hold everything ... why should you follow Weiss Ratings' advice? Another good question ...

The answer? We're not strangers — just ask your librarian. Weiss Ratings has been a trusted friend on library reference shelves for many years.

For more than 30 years, Weiss Ratings has been recognized as a leader in helping consumers manage their finances. When consumers need help deciding which toaster, washing machine, or car to buy, they turn to a consumer protection agency for advice. In the same way, Weiss Ratings has been helping consumers for decades track down and find financially reliable and responsible banks, insurance companies, savings and loans, HMOs, and other financial institutions. In fact, we've become known as "America's Consumer Advocate for Financial Safety."

We strive to put the words of our mission statement into practice every day:

Weiss Ratings, Inc. Mission Statement

"Our mission is to empower consumers, professionals, and institutions with high quality information for selecting or monitoring a financial services company or financial investment. In doing so, Weiss Ratings, Inc. will adhere to the highest ethical standards by maintaining our independent, unbiased outlook and approach to advising our customers."

The reason why we're **the** source for you to take into the investing jungle is simply this:

We don't accept compensation from the companies we rate.

We believe that's the main reason we're clearly more accurate than our competition.

We're a rating agency that can speak frankly in pointing out the risks involved. But we're different — we're independent, which means that we don't allow companies to preview ratings or suppress their publication if they're unfavorable. We're not trying to profit by selling you on any one path to take. Instead, we're here to explain all the paths and help protect you from making a bad decision about which path to take.

This chart illustrates how the average return of Weiss' Top-Rated Stocks outperformed the average return of the S&P 500 Index from December 2001 to June 2004.

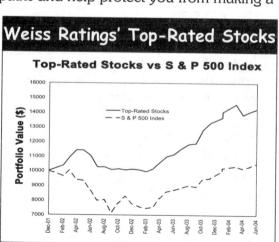

Weiss Ratings' Top-Rated Stocks

Top-Rated Stocks vs S & P 500 Index

Our stock ratings consider both performance and risk, which gives you a balanced evaluation of a stock's earnings prospects. The Weiss Investment Ratings indicate which companies, in our opinion, show enough of the necessary characteristics to make them worthy of your investing dollars — but only once you've studied them thoroughly so you know if they're right for you. How do you know? By understanding risk and return, which is how much you're willing to risk, in exchange for how much you need or want to earn — and how these fit your investing goals and your own personal tolerance for risk. Don't worry! We'll guide you through this step by step!

The recession and bear market of 2000 through 2002 taught stock investors that there are no guarantees that stocks will always increase in value. Understanding the risk of each investment helps you to make good decisions, regardless of what happens in the market. In the three-year bear market, if you had followed Weiss Ratings' advice, your wallet would have been safe through one of the most volatile and upsetting periods of time in investing history.

Take a look again at the chart on page 4 and see the profitable "high road" that Weiss Ratings provided to its followers from December 2001 through June 2004. Readers who followed our advice through those years consistently and substantially beat the S&P 500 Index. Most importantly, they also didn't fall off the cliff during the 2002 crash!

The lessons you'll learn in this book — along with the specific stocks that we'll recommend — will help you keep up with the market and begin to profit, as you start applying what you're learning to earning! Our company has helped thousands of consumers make sound, informed financial decisions since 1971 — and we'd like to help you too.

Weiss Ratings Performance	
Stocks Rated	% of Stocks with Positive 1 Yr Return*
A	92.09%
B	86.39%
C	81.86%
D	69.30%
E/F	60.82%
S & P 500	87.02%

*Based on subsequent one year total return for stocks rated on 07/16/04

The chart shows the percentage of stocks with a positive one-year return for each letter grade category that Weiss assigns to stocks.

Be Wise — Look Ahead!

"This all sounds very nice — but why bother?" you ask. I have Social Security, Medicare, and a little cash to count on in my Golden Years.

For awhile now, the federal government has been sending a message loud and clear: you can't count on Social Security to pay all — or any! — of your living expenses when you retire. In addition, health care costs are rising into the nosebleed zone. According to the 2003 study conducted by the Kaiser Family Foundation, a nonprofit organization that studies health care issues, and Hewitt Associates, a consulting firm, 10% of all large employers cut health benefits in 2002 for future retirees and another 20% say they are likely to end health benefits for future retirees in the next three years[1]. The handwriting is on the wall: you've got to be prepared to take care of yourself.

But the good news is — the government is encouraging retirement investing by setting up tax shelters known as tax-deferred retirement plans. These are gifts from our government [401(k)s, 403(b)s, Individual Retirement Accounts (IRAs), Keoghs, etc.].

So whether you're a young person who wants to save for retirement, or a mature person trying to maintain a livable income, learning to invest in the stock market can help you reach your goals. You may want to help your child go to the college of his or her choice, or buy a new home. Investing in the stock market can help you fund these goals, too.

No Time Like the Present!

"I'm still not sure — the news is pretty discouraging lately. Is there a good time to get into the stock market?"

Any time is a good time to invest in stocks as long as you do it intelligently. It's the nature of the stock market to be up one day and down the next. But you shouldn't follow performance too closely — that may confuse and ultimately discourage you.

So now we have a question for you: what if there was a tried-and-true way of investing?

[1]Kaiser Family Foundation and Hewitt Associates, Retiree Health Benefits Now and in the Future, January 2004.

There is! The key to stock investing success is self-education and self-management. The rewards are worth it if you look at the stock market's track record: from 1925 to 2003, investors who owned stocks in large companies earned an average of 10.4% each year — nearly twice as much as bonds.

Wise Guide Keeps You on Track

To educate yourself and manage your own investments successfully, we'll give you lots of advice and information in this book. Be on the lookout for our "Wise Guide," who pops up frequently with advice and timely warnings.

Don't Get Lost

These signs will highlight tips and techniques for finding your way through the financial jungle so you don't get lost and veer off the track:

Be On The Lookout:
Alerts you to the dangers you may encounter on your investing journey.

Survival Tip:
Leads you to tips, rules and techniques to follow to ensure a successful trip.

Deserves Another Look:
Discover important highlights, good news, and things to celebrate along the way.

We'll also be referring to **www.MartinWeiss.com**, which is loaded with lots of helpful information — and it's FREE! All you have to do is register. This website is easy to use, even for the most technologically challenged. Most of all, it's fun, because you're learning how to take control.

You'll even be able to attend a few courses at "Investors University," virtually speaking. There's a glossary of investing terms and some simple calculators to help you do the math on esti-

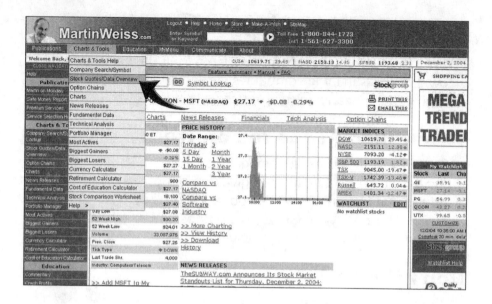

mating how much you want to fund your goals, and then, how much risk you take to earn the returns you need. For example, from the top menu bar under "Charts & Tools," (**www.MartinWeiss.com**), place your mouse on "Stock Quotes/Data Overview" and enter a company's ticker symbol. Here you can view a snapshot of the market, the latest company news releases, and a summary of the stock "fundamentals", or key characteristics, that make the company deserving of your investing dollars. Finally, you can walk step-by-step through setting up your own portfolio and learn how to track its performance.

So don't be a victim — and don't get caught short. Take control of your own financial future by learning to blaze your own trail through the investing jungle successfully!

Part I

Know the Jungle

- **Understanding Stock Basics**
- **Exploring Market Indices**
- **Diversifying Your Portfolio**

Chapter 1

Lions and Tigers and Bears ... OH MY!

W hen you step into the investing jungle, what will you find there? Lions (stocks), and tigers (bonds), and bears (cash), for sure. But they're not as scary as you think — if you're traveling with our Wise Guide.

These three are the main investment classes, but the one we'll be tracking exclusively in this book is the king of the jungle: stocks.

We're going to immediately start pointing out what we see as we head down the trail on our safari, but you can also turn to the glossary for a quick review of any boldface terms used in the book.

You may have heard **stocks** referred to as **equities** or **securities**. The reason they're called equities is that you purchase an equity, or ownership, share of a company. Stock is also called a security for the same reason, because you're securing a share of ownership in the company. That's right; you'll be a business owner just like you've always dreamed! But, as you know from everyday life, there are terrifically run businesses and there are businesses that make you say, "I'll never go back there again!" How do you know the difference before you buy the stock? That's what this guided tour will be teaching you.

So when you buy stock, you become part owner of the company — maybe only a very small part, but still, an owner. The

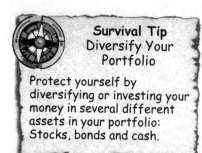

Survival Tip
Diversify Your
Portfolio

Protect yourself by diversifying or investing your money in several different assets in your portfolio: Stocks, bonds and cash.

size of the part you own, by the way, is irrelevant to your personal objectives.

We won't cover bonds in this book, but it's important for you to know that they're out there in the investing jungle. When you buy a bond, you don't become part owner of a company — you're the bank! You lend the company, or others, money. When companies, counties, municipalities, or the U.S. government need to raise money, but not raise taxes or prices, they have bond offerings.

Bonds are loans, with a maturity date, and a percentage rate, promised to you, the Bank of I.O.U.! The maturity date and set percentage rate can make bonds an attractive investment as part of a stabilizing influence in your investment portfolio. But you don't want just bonds in your portfolio — over the long haul, stocks outperform bonds. If you want to purchase and own bonds, it's very important to have quality bonds in your portfolio. See our *Weiss Ratings' Guide to Bond and Money Market Mutual Funds* at your local library if you want to continue to learn about bonds.

When financial advisors suggest you **diversify,** or vary your investments, they're advising you to spread out any potential **risk,** or decline, in your investment portfolio. Your investment **portfolio** is a collection of all of your investments, which could include assets from each of these three classes. It's like a nutritionist telling you to eat a little bit of each type of food to maximize your health. A balance of green vegetables, lean meats, dairy products, and whole grain breads keep you physically and mentally healthy. Likewise, you want to invest your money in a variety of assets in your portfolio: stocks, bonds, and cash products. Cash investments include products like Certificates of Deposit (CDs) and money market mutual funds that keep you financially healthy.

Ready then? Get out your compass.

Chapter 2

Which Type of Stock Should You Pick?

Wow, our jeep just rounded a clearing, and there they are — a pride of lions (stocks). Glad we're looking at them from a distance! It's interesting — there seems to be two really different types, of different sizes and coloring. Yes, the Wise Guide says, we're actually seeing double — the two types of lions we're looking at are preferred stocks and common stocks.

They both look awesome. "What's the difference?" you ask our Guide.

Remember, regardless of which type of stock you buy, purchasing stock makes you a part owner, or **shareholder**, of a company.

Let's begin with preferred stock.

Companies that sell **preferred stock** are actually offering a blend of a more aggressive investment (stock) and a more conservative one (bond). This combination means that the price of preferred stock does not fluctuate as much as the price of common stock. That's

Deserves Another Look
Preferred Stock Benefits

The main benefit to owning preferred stock is that the investor has a greater claim on the company's assets than common stockholders. Preferred stockholders always receive their dividends first and, in the event the company goes bankrupt, preferred stockholders are paid off before common stockholders.

why many risk-adverse investors favor preferred stock.

Another advantage to owning preferred stock is that it almost always pays a dividend to shareholders.

Preferred stock also offers these benefits:

Companies pay dividends to preferred stock shareholders *before* they pay dividends to common stock shareholders.

Dividends accumulate if the company's board of directors decides to put a freeze on divvying up profits because it doesn't have the financial resources.

If the company goes bankrupt, preferred stockholders have a claim to any assets ahead of common stockholders.

On the other hand, preferred stockholders don't have any voting rights. To many investors, this doesn't really matter, but if, as an owner, you are passionate about management decisions at the company, you may want the right to vote. If so, then preferred stock is not for you.

Now let's talk about **common stock**.

Common stock, which is sold by most companies, is the only "pure" form of stock in the market. It's what people are talking about when they just mention "stocks." Because common stock has the potential for greater returns, investors buy it more often than preferred stock.

Common stock represents an equity ownership in the company and entitles shareholders the right to vote on management issues at the annual shareholder's meeting.

Common stockholders may, or may not, receive dividends, depending on management's decision about distributing profits.

Many beginning investors think that preferred stock is better than common stock, but that's not necessarily the case. Your decision to purchase one over the other depends upon your financial goals, your tolerance for risk, and your interest in voting rights in the company.

Because most investors are interested in price appreciation, they usually purchase common stock. You get more "bang for your buck." It's that simple — and so is our goal for you: to get the returns you need to fund your dreams. That's why we wrote this book.

So, from this point on, whenever we refer to "stock," we mean common stock. A little later, in Part II, we'll begin learning about the specific kinds of stocks that are best for you: growth-producing or income-producing.

Right now, though, you're ready to step a little further along the trail.

How Do You Make Money Investing In Stock?

There are two ways to earn money when you invest in stock: price appreciation and dividends.

If the company you invest in does well and makes money, its stock becomes attractive to own and soon, more investors will want to own some of the company that you own. That's when supply and demand works in your favor. The greater the demand, the more the price is driven up. The price moving up (because more people are buying the stock) is known as **price appreciation** — your stock increases in value. You'll realize a profit, or gain, when you sell stock that has appreciated.

Say you buy stock for $10 a share, and it grows, or appreciates, to $15. Smart you! You earned $5, and the value of your share of stock increased, or appreciated, by 50%. The flip side of that is price depreciation, which is another way of saying that the price of a stock went down.

In addition to the potential price appreciation, or attractiveness, of your stock in the public's eye, you can also earn a **dividend** when you own stock.

Distributing dividend payments is another way for a company to share its profit with you. This means that each quarter the company pays you a certain amount of money for each share of stock you own. Usually dividend payments are much smaller than the price of the stock. For example, a company whose stock price is $15 per share might pay a dividend of four cents per share each quarter. Many times, dividends come at the expense of greater price appreciation because the company is distributing its profits to shareholders rather than reinvesting these profits back into the growth of the company. However, companies that pay dividends can be very attractive to investors because they offer a steady stream of income.

Whichever you pick — current income (dividends) or longer-term growth (price appreciation) — as your priority depends on what you need. It's that easy.

Getting the hang of this? It's time for a little breather. You've done a good job getting started. There's a nearby lake, and our Wise Guide says it's warm enough to take a dip and cool off.

Chapter 3

What's the Temperature of the Lake Today?

Every night on the evening news, you hear references to the two main stock market indices: the Dow Jones Industrial Average and the S&P 500 Index ("indices" is the plural of "index"). Now you ask, "Why are they so important that we need to hear about them every single night?"

Well, think of the Dow Jones and the S&P 500 indices as big stock market thermometers. That's right; they actually take the temperature of the stock market so you know the condition of the lake.

A **market index** is a group of stocks that share some common characteristics. It's an important tool, because it helps you figure out how your stock is doing, compared to its peers. So you've got to use the right one to take your stock's temperature. Let's start by looking at the various thermometers, or indices, that are available to you.

For example, the S&P 500 is a group of 500 stocks chosen by Standard and Poor's because they have common characteristics, such as their size and popularity, and make up a good representation of the entire stock market. So if you want to know if a stock performs better, or worse, than the

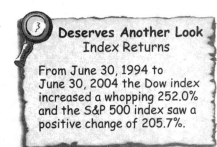

Deserves Another Look
Index Returns

From June 30, 1994 to June 30, 2004 the Dow index increased a whopping 252.0% and the S&P 500 index saw a positive change of 205.7%.

Leading Indicator	What Is It?	Good News	Market Response	Bad News	Market Response	Data Released
Consumer confidence data	Reflects how consumers feel about their personal economic situation and expectations for the future	If confidence rises, consumers are more optimistic and likely to spend, especially on big-ticket items. This translates into higher corporate profits.	▲	When confidence falls, consumers are more likely to scrimp than spend, sending stocks down in anticipation of lower profits.	▲	Middle and end of each month
Consumer price index (CPI)	Tells whether the prices of everyday goods and services are rising or falling	When the CPI falls slightly or remains unchanged, consumers will likely be willing to spend more on nonessentials such as entertainment and travel, a positive sign for stocks.	▲	If the index goes up by 0.3% to 0.4% for 3 straight months, consumers will likely spend less. A rising index also foreshadows inflation, causing the Fed to raise short-term interest rates.	▲	Middle of each month
Crude oil prices	Shows whether consumers and industries will have to pay more or less for fuel	A drop in prices at the pump puts more money in consumers' pockets. Though stocks generally rise, oil stocks fall as lower prices depress profits.	▲	When crude increases (or exceeds $35 a barrel) fears about inflation and cash strapped consumers depress stocks. Hard hit will be airlines and trucking.	▲	Fluctuates throughout the day
Dollar's value	Dictates the price of imported and exported goods, from hair spray and wine to cars and clothing	As the dollar's value declines, U.S. products become cheaper abroad, sending stocks of large multinational companies up in anticipation of higher profits.	▲	As the dollar rises in value against foreign currencies, travelers abroad do well but U.S. goods suffer as their prices soar, sending stocks of multinationals down.	▲	Fluctuates throughout the day
Employment report	Indicates the rate at which U.S. companies are hiring new employees	When it's reported that the unemployment rate is falling and that the previous month saw 200,000 or more new hires, consumers feel secure about their jobs and spend more.	▲	If the numbers show less than 100,000 new hires in the previous month and unemployment is rising, consumers become uncertain about their job security and cut spending, sending stocks down.	▲	First Friday of each month

10 Leading Indicators Table

Indicator	Reflects	▲	▼	Released
Housing starts	Reflects the number of new homes being built	If housing starts rise at least 5%, it signals that a wide-ranging spending spree has begun. Building materials, furnishings and many other home-related goods are purchased.	When housing starts begin to fall, it can be a sign that consumer confidence has ebbed. Many industries may begin to cut back in advance of slower consumer spending, sending stocks down.	Middle of each month
Producer price data	Shows whether companies are paying wholesalers more or less for the goods they will turn around and sell to consumers	When these numbers fall or remain flat, companies are paying the same or less for the things they sell, enabling them to hold down prices, sell more goods and boost profits.	A jump in price data means companies must choose between absorbing the loss or passing higher prices along. Either way, profits will be lower, sending stocks down.	A few days before the CPI is released
Purchasing managers data	Reflects the rate of spending by U.S. companies on equipment, employees and other operating must-haves	A rising rate signals businesses are investing more in growth, reflecting optimism in future profits. Expect shares of companies making basic goods to rise.	When rates drop, companies are spending less on growth, reflecting a cautious outlook. Diminished corporate confidence translates into lower profits.	First and third business day of each month
Retail sales	Charts consumer spending at brick-and-mortar and online stores	An upturn indicates consumer confidence. Stocks of big retailers, price clubs and online stores will likely jump.	A decline indicates consumers aren't upbeat about the economy. A persistent decline will depress retailers' stocks.	Middle of each month
Short-term interest rates	Set by the Federal Reserve, these rates dictate what banks charge each other to borrow money	When the Fed cuts short-term rates, longer-term rates tend to fall. As they do, stocks become more attractive than bonds and debt becomes less expensive.	If the Fed hikes short-term rates, longer-term rates often follow. Bonds become more attractive than stocks. Borrowing costs more, and spending declines.	The Fed meets eight times a year to decide on short-term interest rates

Reprinted with permission from Jeremy Siegel, Wharton School of Business overall market, you check this index. You also may check "The Dow," because this index is made up of stock from the 30 largest U.S. companies, which drive the economy, and therefore, many forecasters believe, reflect a pretty accurate picture of the market.

If the stock market appears to be enjoying a positive return on a regular basis and the economic news is sunny, the stock market is enjoying prosperity. But if, on a regular basis, the indices are showing trouble night after night, you may want to investigate where the trouble is coming from. Remember, a down market can pose a buying opportunity or it could be a warning sign of more to come.

You have to investigate further, and find out if the reason is temporary, or here to stay for awhile. That's when investors use additional economic information from several sources to investigate, much of it looking at different aspects of consumer spending, which drives two-thirds of the U.S. economy. These bits of the puzzle can offer clues about how your stock may do under these conditions.

How can you track these changes for yourself? Take a glance at the chart on the previous pages. It's a map that will lead you safely through this particular part of the jungle. The chart shows 10 leading indicators used to measure the strength of the economy and how the market generally responds following positive or negative results of an indicator.

That was refreshing, wasn't it? Now you're ready to paddle a little bit more around the lake.

Check the Benchmark

Just like it's smart to check prices when you're ready to go shopping, it's smart to compare performance when you're ready to shop for stocks. You can do this by comparing the performance of the stock you're interested in with the performance of the stock's market index.

Let's say you went shopping for a pair of hiking boots before you headed into the jungle with our Wise Guide. You're interested in the price of the boots, but you're even more interested in how comfortable they are on your feet — in other words, their performance.

A market index would be comparable to the average level of comfort of all hiking boots (or maybe the 15 styles you tried on). If you decide to buy L.L. Bean boots, you might compare the comfort level of L.L. Bean's boot to the comfort level of all the boots you tried on to decide if L.L. Bean is more or less comfortable (meaning, the boots perform better or worse).

Each index is made up of a group of stocks that have some shared characteristics. So if you're considering a particular stock (or boot), you compare its performance to the average performance of its index (the group of 15 boots you tried on).

Make sense? Market indices are also called **benchmarks**, because they are things you compare individual stocks against to get an idea of how good or bad they are.

What are some of the shared characteristics of an index or group of stocks? They include:

▲ Company size;

▲ Stock liquidity;

▲ Industry ranking and

▲ Diversification.

Company size, for instance, is one important characteristic. Why is it important?

Large companies — "large caps," whose total stock is valued at $5 billion or more in the stock market — usually have greater access to alternative sources of money to support their growth. "Small cap" companies, whose total stock circulating in the market ranges from $250 million to $1 billion, may have trouble borrowing more money or issuing more stock in a time of need. Mid-cap stocks are in between in size.

On the other hand, large corporations are typically more stable than small companies, but their growth prospects are usually more limited because they're already large and don't typically have as much room to grow.

Now let's take a look at a few performance benchmarks and see how they can vary in comparing stock performance because of the characteristics of the stocks included:

Market Index Returns	
Dow Jones Wilshire 5000	19.29%
Russell 2000	33.41%
DJIA	18.62%
S&P 500	19.10%
NASDAQ Composite Index	26.78%
April 2003 – April 2004	

An index's defining characteristic, or characteristics, is the reason why the benchmarks can vary so widely. Let's take a closer look at each of the indices:

Define Your Stock Market Index

The S&P 500 Index

If you're interested in buying stock from a "large-cap" company, meaning companies with the most money circulating in the stock market ($5 billion or more), this is the index you compare it to.

This index, the most widely known, and widely regarded, benchmark of the U.S. equities market, compares the performance of a representative sample of 500 "large-cap" companies in leading industries of the U.S. economy. The S&P 500 is maintained by the S&P Index Committee, whose members include economists and analysts. The committee rates stocks based on how big they are, how liquid, or available their assets are, their rank in their industry, and how diversified they are. The S&P 500 is frequently used as the standard of comparison in determining a stock's investment performance.

The DJIA, or Dow Jones Industrial Average

If you want to buy "blue-chip" stocks, which are stocks known for their ability to make money and pay dividends to shareholders, then this is the index to compare it to.

This index measures 30 "blue-chip" stocks, which get their fancy name from the companies they repre-

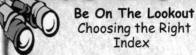

Be On The Lookout
Choosing the Right Index

The S&P 500 is often referred to as "the market," but it's important for you to remember that it may not be the right index to compare your stock against, if the stock you're comparing doesn't have similar characteristics to those 500 companies. Pick the index that compares the characteristics of the stocks you are interested in buying.

sent. These are large, creditworthy companies traded in the U.S., which are famous for their quality and the wide acceptance of their products and services. By studying these companies, many believe you can get a good picture of how the market as a whole is performing.

This index, prepared and published by Dow Jones & Co., is one of the oldest of all the market indicators. The companies within the Dow are widely held by individuals and institutional investors. The Dow's 30 stocks represent about a fifth of the $8 trillion-plus market value of all U.S. stocks, and about a quarter of the value of stocks listed on the New York Stock Exchange. Although there are now dozens of alternatives, the Dow is still the index financial professionals instinctively check first to see how "the market" is doing. It has a wide following among investors, and is well known by even those who have yet to invest in equities.

NASDAQ Composite Index

If you're looking for an index that contains companies whose common characteristic is size, or "market capitalization," measured according to the total dollar value of all outstanding shares, check out this index.

The NASDAQ Composite Index looks at the market capitalization of both domestic and international stocks. Because it is so broad-based, and evaluates more companies (over 4,000) than most other stock market indices, the NASDAQ is also widely followed and quoted among the major market indices.

Russell 3000® Index

If you're looking at a stock from a new and growing company, this is the index to compare it to.

The Russell 3000® Index, which represents 98% of the U.S. market, provides a barometer of the broad market and is revised annually to include new and growing equities.

Russell 2000® Index

If you're looking at stock from a "small-cap" company (a company with a market value less than $1 billion), this is the index to compare it to.

The Russell 2000® Index, which includes the smallest 2000 securities in the Russell 3000, offers investors access to "small-cap" companies. Like the Russell 3000, this index is also revised annually to include this part of the market.

Market Index Characteristics

Index	# of Companies	Avg. Size	Comments
S&P 500	500	Large cap	Widely known index
DJIA	30	Large cap	Includes "blue-chip" stocks from large, creditworthy companies
NASDAQ	4,000+	Various	Broad-based, includes domestic and international
Russell 3000	3000	Various	New and growing companies
Russell 2000	2000	Small-cap	Includes the smallest 2000 securities in the Russell 3000
DJ Wilshire 5000	5000	All	Largest and broadest of U.S. stocks

Dow Jones Wilshire 5000 Index

This index, the largest of the indices, measures the performance of nearly all U.S. companies. This means you could compare any stock to this index, especially those that don't have any of the characteristics of the stocks that make up the other indices.

Whew! It took a lot of paddling to get to the other side of the lake, but you did it. Now you're ready to look at the stock tables published daily in your local newspaper. It gives you a snapshot of useful information to help you further down the trail.

Learn How to Read the Clues

Before you go to the grocery store, you often check prices by looking in your local newspaper. It's the same when you go shopping for stocks: you check the stock tables printed in the business section of your daily newspaper. The tables give you a snapshot of the market by looking at activity on a few of the indices and the **stock exchanges** they trade on. The New York Stock Exchange (NYSE) in Lower Manhattan is the most widely known, and largest, of the stock exchanges, where the nation's largest companies have historically sold their shares.

Don't get overwhelmed by some of the following terms.

Review a sample from the newspaper on the next page, then we'll pull it apart graphically. We define all the terms and label them.

Good job! You're learning how to keep your head in the jungle. Forward!

Total value of index

Advanced: The number of stocks in the exchange that went up during the last business day.

Amount of increase or decrease since the last business day.

Declined: The number of stocks in the exchange that went down during the last business day.

Volume: The number of shares that were traded in the exchange during the last business day.

Market profile

Wilshire 5000
10980.88 +136.64

Russell 2000
578.57 +11.93

NYSE

Unchanged: The number of stocks in the exchange that did not change during the last business day.

53.6M	Advanced 600
12	Declined 278
10	Unchanged 84

Amex
1238.80 +11.65

Volume 293.6M
New Highs 35
New Lows 13

Nasdaq
1976.76 +33.67

Advanced	2353	Volume	1668.1M
Declined	806	New Highs	72
Unchanged	286	New Lows	15

New Highs: The number of stocks for which the price hit a new high during the last business day.

New Lows: The number of stocks for which the price hit a new low during the last business day.

MOST ACTIVE

Name	Volume	Last	Chg.
NortelNw	69,254,100	5.58	+.21
Agere	53,811,900	3.23	-.18
Lucent	49,540,700	3.93	+.08

Name	Volume	Last	Chg.
Nasd100Tr	8		
SPDR	3		
SemiHTr	1		
	2,871,800	3.59	+.19
	2,702,800	29.75	+.34

Most Active: A list of companies on the exchange whose stocks were traded more than anyone else's along with the number of shares that were traded (**Volume**), the last closing price (**Last**), and the amount the share's price changed during the last business day (**Chg.**).

MOST ACTIVE

Name	Volume	Last	Chg.
usS			
cle			
os			
o			
Mic			
Matl	24,646,700	21.32	+.18
Uniph	23,118,500	4.15	+.05
Mamma	19,901,700	10.57	+.79
Yahoo	15,879,700	44.85	+2.28

	HI	Low	Close	Chg.
30 Indus	10326.52	10184.30	10300.30	+115.63
20 Transp	2855.61	2790.04	2847.65	+59.30
15 Utils	281.50	276.23	281.40	+5.20
65 Stocks	2968.48	2919.03	2963.36	+44.63

Standard and Poor's Indexes

Stock	Open	High	Low	Last	Chg.
S&P 100	545.56	552.64	545.56	551.48	+.92
S&P 500	1110.70	1125.76	1110.70	1123.75	+1?
S&P MidCap	588.26	596.44	588.26	596.13	+7.87
S&P SmallCap	276.33	281.70	276.33	281.66	+5.33

Segments of the Dow Jones – Industrials, Transportation, Utilities with the highest level at which each traded at during the last business day, the lowest level, the level at which each closed at the end of the day, and the amount each changed during that day.

Various S&P Indices with the opening amount, the highest level each index traded at during the last business day, the lowest level, the level at which each closed at the end of the day, and the amount each changed during that day.

Chapter 4

Pay Attention!
You're Walking in a Jungle

Remember, you've got to pay attention to the clues when you're on safari. Many beginning investors, unfortunately, get so dazzled by the glitter of the stock market that they lose sight of the trees in the midst of the jungle. We'd like to tell you what happened to one beginning investor — and how to avoid repeating his mistake.

John, a 38-year-old accountant, decided to go into the investing jungle without a guide. He was good at crunching numbers at work, and if he applied that same skill to investing in the stock market, he'd have a chance to win big. After all, a lot of other professionals he knew had made a few bucks in the market.

This was a few years ago, when the stock market began its dizzying ride to the top of what looked like an endlessly blue sky without a cloud in sight. John jumped in with both feet. After sharing his dream of a summer home with his wife, he took his life savings and sunk them into a few carefully chosen technology stocks. He had crunched the numbers, done his research … everything looked good.

Unfortunately, his family's dreams were shattered when the stocks hit rock bottom, wiping out all of his hard-

Survival Tip
Assessing Performance

Comparing your stock's return to the sector's is another way to assess its performance.

earned savings in the blink of an eye.

If John had only joined the safari and taken the tour with our Wise Guide ...

What did John do wrong? What happened?

He didn't follow one very critical rule of investing — diversification. You balance your risk by diversifying, and buying stocks, in different **sectors**, or industries. Sectors can be sliced and diced in many different ways. We slice our stocks into 10 different sectors. A few of the popular ones are technology, health care, and financial services. John's mistake was buying too much of one sector. For a list of sectors, see the chart on this page.

Like too many investors, he believed the hype: nothing but blue skies with those fast-moving tech stocks! But the reality was, when tech stocks fell rapidly, he, and a lot of other investors at the time, got washed out by some unexpected storm clouds.

To stay dry, John should have better understood the **risk/reward** trade-off. In other words, he didn't recognize that all his buddies who were making lots of money investing in tech stocks were also taking on huge amounts of risk. Obviously, more risk than he was prepared to handle. How is risk defined? Risk is the likelihood that a stock's price will go down. The riskier the stock, the more chance it will decrease in price.

Risk and return work together; the risk you are willing to take affects the returns you can earn in the stock market. The higher the risk, the higher the potential reward.

As you walk through the jungle, you'll also hear about **volatility**, which is how risk is often measured. Volatility is how much stocks go up and down. Some stocks are very volatile while some stocks are more stable and consistent. For example, a volatile stock that you purchase at $10 may go up to $20 in a year, but in the meantime dip down to $5. A stable stock you purchase at $10 may only go up to $13 in a year, but will get there steadily by going from $10 to $11 to $12 and so on. Which one would you like to live with?

Why is it so important to think about the risk you're willing to take before you invest? Because you can't decide on **asset allocation**, or how much to invest in each of the assets in your portfolio, without knowing the risk you're comfortable taking. John failed because he didn't take the time to do that. As a result, he gave up on the stock market before he really had the time to become successful.

Beginning investors often make the mistake of overloading, either putting too much into one stock or, as John did, putting everything into the same sector over and over again. John could have avoided his fall by investing in several different sectors, and in several different companies. Why is this so important? Because if you have good diversification, you won't go hungry if one of the pieces (of your investing pie) falls apart!

Don't get dazzled, like John, by looking at just the return side of the equation. Think about how much risk you can take before you start to get uncomfortable.

That's what you're ready to do in Part II, coming up around the next bend. We'll help you look at how much risk you want to take for the returns you want to earn in the market.

You're ready to go deeper into the jungle — getting a grip on how much risk you want to handle. You're still cautious—you've seen a few lions up close, and they've got lots of teeth! But you have a Wise Guide to rely on, and you're learning that you can conquer fear with the right information, a good plan, and discipline.

Deserves Another Look
Retirement Savings

Everything else equal, women tend to lag behind men in retirement savings because they invest too conservatively. Studies have found that women in general direct only half as much of their savings into stocks as men.

Part II

Know the Map

- **Establishing Financial Goals**
- **Discovering Your "Risk Zone"**
- **Saving to Invest**

Chapter 5

You're on a Mission —
YOURS!

U nlike John, Kathleen, a 35-year-old working mother of two, understood that she needed a Guide for her journey into the investing world to be successful. She had listened attentively to the words of wisdom that our Wise Guide had taught her in Part I and was now ready to continue her adventure.

"But first," warned our Guide, "you must decide where you want to go and what you want to see on your safari. Without a map, you'll wander aimlessly, missing the big game and amazing beauty that the jungle has to offer." The same is true of investing!

So, before embarking on the tour, Kathleen thought about where she wanted to go and what she wanted to see from her investments. Her current financial situation and future goals would determine the "map" that she should follow.

What were Kathleen's financial dreams? To have the means to not only send her two young children to college, but to also enjoy her retirement. But how? How could she possibly save enough to accomplish these goals? Many days, Kathleen felt as though she was just barely getting by paycheck to paycheck.

Then she thought about how she had swum across the entire length of that huge lake and learned all about market indices. If she had done that, then she could learn how to pick a good stock and invest wisely. So, first steps first, she listened to our Wise Guide and mapped out her financial goals by writing a mission statement that would keep her on the right path.

Have you ever read the mission statement of a company or organization you admire? Over and over again, you'll notice certain qualities, but there are always the same few that keep topping the list. We call them the three "Ds":

▲ a dream
▲ determination
▲ and discipline

These are the same qualities that you, the beginning investor, can use to be successful, too. Committing words to paper has a funny way of turning thoughts into action. It doesn't matter whether your mission statement is one line or one paragraph; what does matter is how serious, and how prepared, you are in order to reach your goals. Writing a personal mission statement helps you keep going in the right direction.

Kathleen's Mission Statement:

I'm tired of worrying about money. In the next two years, I want to have an emergency fund with six months of savings, in case my car — or job! — collapses, and get rid of the credit card balance I've been carrying since college. In 10 and 15 years, I want to be able to send Harry, now 8, and Amanda, 3, to college. My ex is not in a position to contribute to a college fund, so I will be responsible for all education expenses. I want to think about my "Golden Years" without feeling scared that I won't have enough money to live on. With 30+ years to save, I want to learn how to invest in the stock market, so I'll have enough money to see my dreams come true.

Kathleen has big dreams she wants to fund. By mapping out her goals, she has come to realize something very exciting.

In her case, she has the time to invest in the stock market as a way to reach her goals.

Your Personal Financial Mission Statement

Mission statements keep companies and organizations focused in order to achieve business goals.

People need mission statements too, including you! Why? To help you identify what's important and what you value most in your life. That way, you'll focus your energy on what matters most to you so that you're able to accomplish the things you really want out of life. This is especially true for your financial goals. After all, if you don't know where you want to go, it's unlikely that you'll ever get to your destination.

To create your personal financial mission statement, spend some time thinking about your current situation. Now imagine where you would like to be — financially — next year, five years, and twenty (or more) years from now. Be specific and realistic!

To help you along this journey, here are some ideas for you to consider:

1. Retirement: I would like to retire in _____ years, by the age of _____ and with a portfolio valued at $_____.

2. Rainy Day Savings: I would like to have three to six months worth of expenses, approximately $_____, saved within _____ weeks/months.

3. Education or Business Opportunity: I would like to save for a child's college education, which will cost $_____ by a date of _____.

I would like to have money to enhance my education (graduate school, law school, or a specialized field of study). I will need $_____ within _____ months/years to pursue this dream.

My dream is to open my own business so I will need $_____ in capital by _____.

Are there other opportunities that you would like to plan for the future?

_____

At what cost?

_____

4. Home or Car Purchase: I would like to save a down
payment of $_____ for a new/larger house by
_____.

I would like to save for a second home located in
_____ and have a
$_____ down payment by _____.

I would like to buy a new car within _____ months, which
will cost $_____.

5. Travel / Hobbies: My dream vacation to
_____ in _____ months/years
will cost $_____.

My family enjoys the water so I would like to upgrade our
boat within _____ months/years to a
_____ costing $_____.

What other special interests or activities do you want to
include in your plan?

_____

What is the cost?_____

6. Debt Reduction: I would like to pay down my mortgage
_____ years sooner than it matures.

I would like to reduce personal or credit card debt of
$_____ within _____ months/years.

To achieve your dreams, it's very important that you write
your goals down and refer to them often. Sort them according
to the time frame — short-term versus long-term, because
you will need to save for them differently. Finally, post your
goals so you will have a constant reminder to stay focused!

Everyone's situation is different. For example, different short- and long-term goals (a new car next year compared to a child's college education in seven years to retirement in two decades) need different investing vehicles to achieve different results, or returns. If you're looking at a goal five or more years on the horizon, then investing in the stock market is a smart decision because, despite the risks that can and will occur, you have the potential to earn more money because you have the time you need to ride out the market's ups and downs.

But you're not ready to invest your first dollar until you're much more comfortable with risk and know what you can do to manage it. So let's turn our attention to the next chapter, where we'll walk a little further into the jungle.

Chapter 6

Taming That Animal Called RISK

Once you stare risk in the face, we promise, you won't be scared. To get a grip on risk before it gets a grip on you, ask yourself these four important questions:

1. How Much Risk Can I Handle?

Only as much as you're comfortable losing.

Take on too much risk and you'll panic, selling at the worst possible time. When's that? When you sell low, which is the opposite of tried-and-true investing smarts — buying low and selling high.

Ask yourself: how much am I comfortable potentially losing over a year and still be able to stick to my plan?

> **5% or less?** You have a low tolerance for risk.
> **6%-15%?** You have a moderate tolerance for risk.
> **16%-25%?** You have a high tolerance for risk.

Let's assume you have $10,000 to invest.

If you are comfortable potentially losing only $500, then you have a low tolerance for risk.

If you could handle potentially losing up to $1,500, you have a moderate tolerance for risk.

You have a high tolerance for risk if you could accept losing up to $2,500.

2. How Do I Balance Risk Against My Expectations?

Don't take on more than you can handle. There's always a trade-off with risk — the greater the uncertainty, the greater the potential for higher returns. Stay in your own personal risk zone, regardless of what the market does.

3. How Can I Reduce My Risk?

In real estate, it's location, location, location. In stock investing, it's diversify, diversify, diversify. To reduce your risk, it's smart to invest in all the major asset categories (stocks, bonds, and cash), which are affected by different economic and market factors. You can also spread your risk by diversifying further in each asset category. In the stock category, for example, you diversify by choosing stocks in several different industries. Choose just one stock and you can wipe out your entire portfolio if that one stock decreases in value. Choose several in various industries, so that when one goes down, others will stay put, or go up, and balance out your total performance.

4. How Can Risk Reward Me?

With more money! Historically, the stock market has earned more returns for investors than bonds or cash. And over time, that difference adds up to a lot of money.

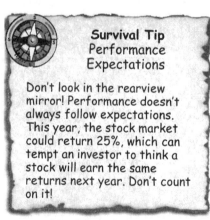

Survival Tip
Performance
Expectations

Don't look in the rearview mirror! Performance doesn't always follow expectations. This year, the stock market could return 25%, which can tempt an investor to think a stock will earn the same returns next year. Don't count on it!

"Risk" isn't sounding too scary to Kathleen after all. Now she's ready to take our Investor Profile Quiz, which will help her figure out the risk she wants to take.

Chapter 7

What's Your Investing Speed: Slow and Steady — or *Smokin'*?

E ach person approaches his or her invest-ment decisions from a unique perspective: theirs! A stock investment that's perfect for someone else may be totally wrong for you, depending on several factors:

▲ How much risk you're comfortable taking,

▲ How much return you expect from your investment,

▲ How much you pay in taxes,

▲ How old you are and

▲ How many years you have to achieve your goal(s).

Investing is all about risk and return; you can't get a handle on one (return) without knowing more about the other (risk).

How fast do you want to go as you head down the trail? Slow (conservative), steady (moderate), or fast (aggressive)? The following quiz helped Kathleen understand her investing speed, and it can help you too. The number at the end of this quiz will tell you how much risk you're willing to take for the returns you need to earn to reach your goals.

> **Survival Tip**
> **Risk Tolerance**
>
> Don't invest a single dollar in the stock market until you decide on the risk you're comfortable taking. Your level of risk tolerance will help determine which stocks you choose to achieve your goals.

The challenge is turning numbers into action, of course. Expectations, colored by our emotions, often get in the way.

As Kathleen reads through each question, she circles the one answer she feels most accurately describes her current point of view. There are no "correct" answers to this quiz, only answers that help you figure out the investment speed that fits your style. Don't worry about how others might view your answers — this is for your eyes only! But it's important to be as honest and accurate as possible.

Ready to get a handle on the risk and return that's right for you? Let's go to the quiz.

Beginner Investor Quiz

	Points	Score
1. I expect I will need to liquidate some or all of my investments in:		
a. 2 years or less	0	
b. 2 to 5 years	5	
c. 5 to 10 years	8	
d. 10 years or more	10	
2. My age group is:		
a. Under 30	10	
b. 30 to 44	9	
c. 45 to 60	7	
d. 61 to 74	5	
e. 75 and older	1	
3. I have a cash reserve equal to 3 to 6 months expenses.		
a. Yes	10	
b. No	1	
4. My primary source of income is:		
a. Salary/other earnings	7	
b. Earnings from my investment portfolio	5	
c. Retirement pension/Social Security	3	
5. I will need regular income from this investment now or in the near future.		
a. Yes	6	
b. No	10	
6. If the stock market were to suddenly decline by 15%, which of the following would most likely be your reaction?		
a. I should have left the market long ago, at the first sign of trouble.	3	
b. I should have substantially exited the stock market by now to limit my exposure.	5	
c. I'm still in the stock market but I've got my finger on the trigger.	7	
d. I'm staying fully invested so I'll be ready for the next bull market.	10	
	Sub Total	

	Points	Score
7. Over the long run, I expect this investment to average returns of:		
a. 8% annually or less	0	
b. 8% to 12% annually	6	
c. 12% to 15% annually	8	
d. 15% to 20% annually	10	
e. Over 20% annually	18	
8. The best way to protect my investment when stock prices are falling is:		
a. To time my purchases and sales of stocks to avoid large losses.	4	
b. To invest in stocks now to take advantage when prices start to rise.	10	
9. The worst loss I would be comfortable accepting on my investment is:		
a. Less than 5%. Stability is very important.	1	
b. 5% to 10%. Modest declines are acceptable.	3	
c. 10% to 15%. There may be losses in the short-run, but over the long-term, higher risk investments will offer higher returns.	8	
d. Over 15%. You don't get high returns without taking risk. I'm looking for maximum capital gains and understand that my investment can substantially decline.	15	
10. The best strategy to employ when stock prices are falling is:		
a. Liquidate stocks and hold cash instead.	10	
b. Use more sophisticated trading techniques to make a profit as prices decline.	7	
c. Wait it out because the market will eventually recover.	5	
11. I would classify myself as:		
a. A buy-and-hold investor who rides out all the peaks and valleys.	10	
b. A market timer who wants to capture the major bull markets.	7	
c. A market timer who wants to avoid the major bear markets.	5	
	Sub Total	

	Points	Score
12. My attitude regarding trading activity is:		
a. Active trading is costly and unproductive.	0	
b. I don't mind frequent trades as long as I'm making money.	2	
c. Occasional trading is okay but too much activity is not good.	1	
13. If the S&P 500 advanced strongly over the last 12 months, my investment should have:		
a. Grown even more than the market.	10	
b. Approximated the performance of the broad market.	5	
c. Focused on reducing the risk of loss in a bear market, even if it meant giving up some upside potential in the bull market.	2	

14. I have experience with the following types of investments.	Extensive	Some	None	
a. U.S. stocks or stock mutual funds	2	1	0	
b. International stock funds	2	1	0	
c. Bonds or bond funds	1	0	0	
d. Futures and/or options	5	3	0	
e. Managed futures or funds	3	1	0	
f. Real estate	2	1	0	
g. Private hedge funds	3	1	0	
h. Privately managed accounts	2	1	0	

15. Excluding my primary residence, this investment represents ____% of my investment holdings.	Points	Score
a. Less than 5%	10	
b. 5% to 10%	7	
c. 10% to 20%	5	
d. 20% to 30%	3	
e. 30% or more	1	

Sub Total	
Sub Total page 43	
Sub Total page 44	
TOTAL	

Add the points in the "Your Score" column to get your total. This score will tell you what risk category you currently fall into. Find the category below that matches your total score. Each category gives a description of the types of investments suitable for your risk tolerance.

Under 58 pts – Very Conservative

You are not willing to accept the risk involved in aiming for a very high return. You don't want to take much risk at all — your primary goal is to keep as much of your money as possible. As a result, most stocks may be a little too risky for your taste, especially in a turbulent market environment. We recommend you stick to the safest bond funds and money market mutual funds where your income stream is predictable and more secure. For information about these types of funds, look for *Weiss Ratings' Guide to Bond & Money Market Mutual Funds,* which can be found in many public libraries. Honestly, it may be best for you not to invest in the stock market after all.

58 to 77 pts – Conservative

You are willing to accept a small amount of risk to aim for good returns, but you're more concerned about minimizing the risk to your principal than you are about maximizing your returns. Don't worry, there are plenty of good stocks that offer strong returns with low risk. For an example of some of Weiss' top-performing stocks with the best risk rating, turn to page 90, Table 7.

78 to 108 pts – Moderate

You're prepared to take on a little added risk to increase your investment returns. This is probably the most common investing approach. To select a stock investment matching your style, turn to page 56, Table 1, where you can find top-performing stocks receiving a risk rating in the fair range.

109 to 129 pts – Aggressive

You appear to be ready to ride out almost any financial storm on your way toward maximizing your investment returns. You understand that the only way to make large returns on your investments is by taking on added risk, and your personal situation seems to allow for that approach. For a selection of high-performing stocks with a risk rating in the weak range, turn to page 57.

Over 129 pts – Very Aggressive

Based on your responses, you appear to be leaning heavily toward speculation. Your primary concern is maximizing your investment growth, and you seem prepared to take on as much risk as necessary in order to do so. Turn to Table 4 on page 59, where you'll find an example of the highest-performing stocks with a risk rating in the very weak range. These investments can be extremely volatile and susceptible to any one of a number of factors. But, they are highly speculative investments that could provide superior results if you can stomach the volatility and uncertainty.

Because she is funding two goals, Kathleen takes the test twice. She's willing to take some risk for herself, which makes her a moderate investor, but little, or none at all, to save for her children's educations, which also makes her a conservative investor. Later in this section, she'll find out how choosing different levels of risk influences the returns she needs to reach her goals.

Kathleen needs to keep her risk scores in mind whenever she thinks about buying a stock. It will be her best tool in choosing the stock investments that are right for her. Knowing your risk tolerance is critical. You can't do

> **Survival Tip**
> **Stay Focused**
>
> **Keep cool.**
>
> **Keep your emotions in check.** Think about investing your money as a business.
>
> **Keep on track.** Review your plan regularly.

a good job in deciding on your portfolio's asset allocation without it.

Chapter 8

Find the Hidden Treasure in RISK

Kathleen's beginning to get a handle on the numbers, and she's excited. She's realizing how the risk she's willing to take affects the returns she'd like to earn to fund her dreams.

To get a handle on the money she'll need, she looks at two calculators on **www.MartinWeiss.com**, one specifically designed for calculating education costs and one for retirement needs. They're really simple to use. Log on to **www.MartinWeiss.com**, and register (for FREE!), under the top menu bar go to the "Charts & Tools" tab and

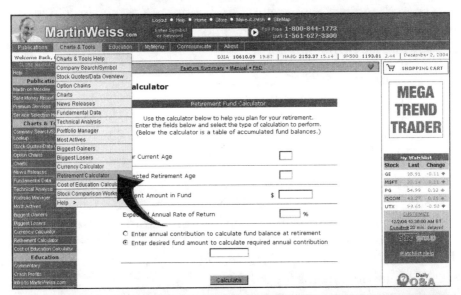

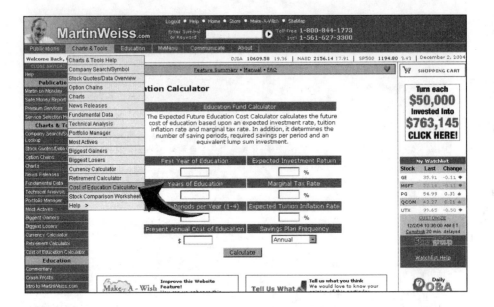

then point to the calculator you wish to use. Click on your choice of the Retirement, Cost of Education or Currency Conversion Calculators.

These simple tools will help you come up with a few key numbers. Say you want to fund education costs in 10 and 15 years, and retirement in 30 years, which are Kathleen's goals.

For retirement, Kathleen thinks about what she currently has saved ($30,000), and what she can save annually ($3,000). Then she thinks about return, and chooses 8%, because that sounds neither too conservative nor too aggressive. And she's surprised by what happens:

Current age	35
Expected age of retirement	65
Current amount in fund	$30,000
Expected rate of return	8%
Annual contribution to fund balance	$3,000

If she saves $3,000 a year at 8% a year, Kathleen will have $687,196 when she retires. She's beginning to feel relieved. Retirement doesn't seem like an impossible dream after all. What if she wants to hit the million dollars that forecasters say retirees need? She increases her anticipated rate of return to 10%, and ends up with an amazing $1,134,808.

Now let's see what the price tag looks like for her children's educations:

A key number used by education calculators is the present annual cost of education, which the calculator uses to project future costs. First Kathleen has to decide what type of school she really has in mind, but when she enters the current annual cost of attending such a college, she is almost speechless.

There's a big difference in price tags. According to the College Board (www.collegeboard.com), a nonprofit organization that tracks college costs and student aid, these are the average annual costs for 2003-2004:

- Four-year private college $19,710
- Four-year public college $4,694
- Two-year public college $1,905

These are only averages. According to the College Board, 70% of students that attend a four-year college pay less than $8,000 for tuition and fees and 43% of those attending two-year colleges pay less than $2,000 per year.

The average total price tag per year including room and board looks like this:

- Four-year private college $26,854
- Four-year public college $10,636

So let's look at the future projected costs of going to a four-year public school (currently $10,636) for both Harry and Amanda assuming a 5% rate of inflation:

- In 2014 $74,672
- In 2019 $95,303
- **Total:**   **$169,975**

To fund these projected costs, Kathleen would have to save $560.14, assuming an 8% investment return, each month until the children start college. There are lots of calculators you can consult, from the College Board, the federal Department of Education, and many others, but they will all give you the same discouraging numbers.

Don't Take the Wrong Turn!

Right about now, due to a sudden attack of CPGS (Chronic Parental Guilt Syndrome), Kathleen is thinking that, okay, she can raid or borrow against her 401(k) to fund her kids' education. Isn't that a good thing to do if she loves her children?

No! Absolutely not! Don't go there! Don't stop funding your retirement to pay for a child's future education costs.

Get a handle on CPGS. Don't expect to pay for everything. You don't have to. Let your child contribute. It's good training for the future, and a head start down the road of taking financial responsibility. Also, financial aid is available to most families. According to the College Board, about half of all college students receive grant aid from some source.

We'd like to offer a different approach:

Look at the Map This Way

Aim to fund a reasonable amount for education, and begin thinking of education as an investment in your child's future. In our opinion, a better way to get a handle on college costs is just deciding how much you can contribute. In Kathleen's case, if she could only contribute a total of $250 a month for both funds, her projected total savings would be roughly half of the expected cost — about $85,000. She should plan that the remainder of the college expenses will be covered with current income while the kids are in college and contributions from her kids who will work to help pay the expenses. $85,000

Be On The Lookout
Education IRAs

ONE WARNING:
Education IRAs (now Coverdell), and also custodial accounts in a child's name, reduce every dollar of financial aid your child receives by 35%. Prepaid tuition plans reduce aid dollar for dollar.

— Not a bad college fund at all!

Kathleen can also start thinking about leveraging tax-deferred dollars to save for her children's education. The choices:

Coverdell Education Savings Accounts (previously Education Individual Retirement Accounts) are investment accounts sponsored by the federal government that pay for "qualified higher education expenses" (tuition, room, board, and supplies). Contributions are not tax-deductible, but earnings are not currently taxed, and withdrawals are tax-free. Maximum contribution: $2,000 a year per student.

State Savings Plans. Earnings are federally tax exempt and most states exempt earnings from state tax. Some states allow families to deduct the full or partial amount of contribution from their state income tax.

Every state now offers one, or both, of the two types that are available. They work the same way: You pay for the cost of tomorrow's college with today's dollars.

Prepaid plans vary from state to state, but typically pay for the cost of attending in-state public universities and community colleges. Most states give you the choice of funding a payment plan or making a lump sum payment. You don't always have to reside in the state to which you prepay tuition, although the future student is generally required to be either a current resident, or have lived in the state and then moved.

These plans, called "529" plans because they get their name from Code 529 of the tax law, allow benefactors (parents, grandparents, relatives) to contribute money into an account set up for a student. These programs work like a mutual fund, with investors' funds pooled and managed by

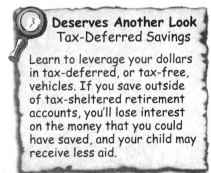

Deserves Another Look
Tax-Deferred Savings

Learn to leverage your dollars in tax-deferred, or tax-free, vehicles. If you save outside of tax-sheltered retirement accounts, you'll lose interest on the money that you could have saved, and your child may receive less aid.

a professional. Whatever you contribute (limits vary according to the state), plus any earnings, can be withdrawn tax-free if it pays for qualified higher education expenses of the designated student. States offer different plans. Check the College Savings Plans Network website (www.collegesavings.org) or call 877-277-6496 for more information.

Not too bad, Kathleen's thinking. She's comfortable with the idea of taking a little more risk to fund her dreams. So now she's ready to look at the next clue — finding the right stocks to start funding her dreams.

Chapter 9

How *Fast* (Growth) or *Slow* (Income) Will You Go?

L ess risk, less reward. This trade-off describes **income stocks**. These are stocks that pay high and regular dividends to shareholders. Some industries known for income-producing stocks include gas, electric, telephone utilities, real estate investment trusts, banks, and insurance companies. High-quality income stocks have a long history of paying dividends, and in many cases, have a track record of regularly increasing dividends.

With **growth stocks**, it's the opposite trade-off: More risk, more reward. These stocks offer the greatest potential for growth, but rarely pay dividends because profits are put right back into the company, rather than paid out directly to shareholders. Therefore, the payoff comes when you sell the stock. Investors buy these stocks because their potential for growth is greater. Growth investors look at the rate at which a business is growing when deciding whether to buy its stock. Normally investors buy shares of new companies, new industries, and new markets that are capable of increasing earnings, and other key factors that we'll study throughout Part III.

Kathleen wants to choose growth stocks to fund her children's education costs. Typically, the most common investment strategy considers age in deciding which stocks to invest in. The younger a child is, the more aggressive a parent can be with the investments, because the ups and downs of the market can be ridden out. As the child gets older and closer to going to college, the investment mix becomes less risky. Kathleen would keep 80% or more in stocks when her children are young, then shift to 50% or 60% in stocks as they enter high school. Finally, when they are ready for college, she would reduce her asset allocation on stocks to 25%.

Regardless of the benefits, Kathleen isn't comfortable taking a lot of risk to fund her children's education. She's not sure she wants to put her money into a state college plan. Right now, she wants to create her own plan so she can have control over it, and she definitely wants to be more conservative with the risk she takes.

So let's look at a sample of some moderate growth stocks in Table 1 that would do well to meet Kathleen's education goals

Table 1: Moderate Growth Stocks

(See Appendix E for a description of each column.)

Company Name	Stock Ticker Symbol	Overall Weiss Investment Rating	Stock Price as of 07/16/04	1-Year Total Return (%) / Percentile	3-Year Total Return (%) / Percentile	Earnings per Share $
ATRION CORP	ATRI	A	43.75	42.46 / 69	24.09 / 77	2.96
BIOMET Inc.	BMET	A	47.65	71.49 / 81	23.60 / 77	1.27
C H ROBINSON WORLDWIDE Inc.	CHRW	A+	45.17	25.75 / 55	14.10 / 62	1.37
CERADYNE Inc.	CRDN	A-	38.51	167.86 / 93	99.73 / 98	0.97
CHICAGO PIZZA & BREWERY Inc.	CHGO	A-	14.30	28.01 / 57	41.01 / 89	0.27
CLAIRES STORES Inc.	CLEKA	A	22.00	68.13 / 79	42.97 / 90	1.29
COACH Inc.	COH	A-	45.87	70.14 / 80	72.51 / 96	1.23
COTT CORP QUE	COT	A-	32.80	44.47 / 70	28.86 / 82	1.19
DXP ENTERPRISES Inc.	DXPE	A-	4.43	119.51 / 89	47.58 / 91	0.53
EXPEDITORS INTL WASH Inc.	EXPD	A	48.87	32.39 / 61	21.14 / 73	1.23
FASTENAL CO	FAST	A	54.74	58.22 / 76	18.51 / 69	1.23
FORWARD AIR CORP	FWRD	A-	36.26	31.22 / 60	12.47 / 59	1.28
HARMAN INTERNATIONAL INDS	HAR	A+	88.55	112.91 / 88	63.49 / 95	1.99
HEADWATERS Inc.	HDWR	A-	23.74	68.13 / 79	43.55 / 90	1.75
MICHAELS STORES Inc.	MIK	A	55.09	45.09 / 70	43.26 / 90	2.76
MULTIMEDIA GAMES Inc.	MGAM	A-	26.33	86.21 / 84	63.87 / 95	1.20
NOVAMERICAN STEEL Inc.	TONS	A-	24.47	201.25 / 94	66.57 / 95	3.83
PATTERSON COMPANIES Inc.	PDCO	A-	72.70	49.09 / 72	27.27 / 80	2.20
PLANTRONICS Inc.	PLT	A-	40.01	61.89 / 77	25.16 / 78	1.39
ROCKWELL AUTOMATION	ROK	A	36.20	39.45 / 67	32.97 / 85	1.77
STRYKER CORP	SYK	A+	55.81	54.31 / 74	27.56 / 80	1.22
UNIFIRST CORP	UNF	A	28.89	13.84 / 42	20.89 / 73	1.74
VSE CORP	VSEC	A	19.50	56.90 / 75	42.87 / 90	1.04
WHOLE FOODS MARKET Inc.	WFMI	A	92.31	81.45 / 83	42.48 / 90	2.10
WRIGLEY (WM) JR CO	WWY	A-	63.29	15.80 / 45	9.07 / 53	2.04

Data date 07/16/04. For the most recent version of this list, please visit www.WeissRatings.com, go to "Products" and click on "Stocks."

for her children. Then, on Table 2, let's look at examples of some slightly more aggressive growth stocks that would be more appropriate for her retirement goals:

Table 2: Moderate/Aggressive Growth Stocks

(See Appendix E for a description of each column.)

Company Name	Stock Ticker Symbol	Overall Weiss Investment Rating	Stock Price as of 07/16/04	1-Year Total Return (%) / Percentile	3-Year Total Return (%) / Percentile	Earnings per Share $
BRASCAN CORP -CL A	BNN	B	28.46	75.82 / 82	34.50 / 86	1.70
CANADIAN NATURAL RESOURCES	CNQ	B	31.77	65.25 / 78	30.24 / 83	3.62
CATAPULT COMMUNICATIONS CORP	CATT	B	20.15	63.13 / 78	4.63 / 46	0.63
CEDAR FAIR -LP	FUN	B	30.90	24.58 / 54	22.79 / 75	1.73
CERES GROUP Inc.	CERG	B-	5.96	91.59 / 85	13.96 / 62	0.63
CHELSEA PROPERTY GROUP Inc.	CPG	B	65.00	59.03 / 76	42.44 / 90	2.33
CHOICE HOTELS INTL Inc.	CHH	B	49.90	74.00 / 81	30.12 / 83	2.06
DHB INDUSTRIES Inc.	DHB	B	14.51	218.92 / 95	83.28 / 97	0.40
DIGITAL RIVER Inc.	DRIV	B	28.50	40.82 / 68	92.75 / 97	0.68
EBAY Inc.	EBAY	A-	83.78	44.55 / 70	44.84 / 91	0.84
ENBRIDGE Inc.	ENB	B-	37.59	7.41 / 36	15.92 / 65	3.20
ENTERTAINMENT PROPERTIES TR	EPR	B-	36.10	29.02 / 58	36.54 / 87	1.88
EVERTRUST FINL GROUP Inc.	EVRT	B-	25.40	54.99 / 75	38.08 / 88	1.01
J2 GLOBAL COMMUNICATIONS Inc.	JCOM	B	27.13	6.92 / 35	150.78 / 99	1.63
LABOR READY Inc.	LRW	B	14.59	87.95 / 84	44.49 / 91	0.54
LIFECELL CORP	LIFC	B	10.73	114.31 / 88	63.07 / 95	0.85
NAM TAI ELECTRONICS	NTE	B	20.94	41.32 / 68	77.86 / 97	0.97
PACTIV CORP	PTV	B	24.17	24.34 / 54	14.37 / 63	0.96
PROVINCE HEALTHCARE CO	PRV	B	16.80	43.83 / 69	-13.61 / 26	0.93
SCP POOL CORP	POOL	B	46.17	79.15 / 83	36.61 / 87	1.51
SHUFFLE MASTER Inc.	SHFL	B	32.29	65.72 / 79	40.52 / 89	0.78
STRATASYS Inc.	SSYS	B	23.13	-15.32 / 19	97.18 / 98	0.73
TALX CORP	TALX	B	23.23	-2.78 / 27	-6.88 / 32	0.92
TRACTOR SUPPLY CO	TSCO	B	40.49	43.75 / 69	98.29 / 98	1.62
YAHOO Inc.	YHOO	B	30.11	81.21 / 83	65.55 / 95	0.25

Data date 07/16/04. For the most recent version of this list, please visit www.WeissRatings.com, go to "Products" and click on "Stocks."

Let's look at a few other scenarios. If Kathleen is within five years of retirement, she would want to look closely at income-producing stocks and consider investing in high-dividend yield stocks, a favorite investment for this age group. In addition to providing a regular stream of income, dividends offer a cushion to investors in bear markets and a source of stability during bull markets.

With the recent change in tax treatment for dividend payments, these stocks are becoming increasingly attractive for all investors, not just retirees. The maximum tax on capital gains, which is the tax you pay on your earnings, has dropped so that the most you'll pay is 15%, but it could be as low as 5%.

If you want to buy dividend-paying stocks, the following chart lists the top contenders based on our research as of 07/16/04. We re-evaluate these stocks every month, so for the most recent list, please visit www.WeissRatings.com, go to "Products" and click on "Stocks."

Table 3: High-Dividend Yielding Stocks

(See Appendix E for a description of each column.)

Company Name	Stock Ticker Symbol	Overall Weiss Investment Rating	Stock Price as of 07/16/04	1-Year Total Return (%) / Percentile	3-Year Total Return (%) / Percentile	Earnings per Share $	Div. Yield	Div. Rate
KNIGHTSBRIDGE TANKERS LTD	VLCCF	B+	32.66	321.06 / 97	41.95 / 90	3.21	13.48	4.40
PETROFUND ENERGY TRUST	PTF	B-	11.66	50.96 / 73	34.42 / 86	0.75	12.86	1.50
AMERICAN MTG ACCEP CO	AMC	B-	14.35	-2.08 / 28	8.73 / 53	1.45	11.66	1.67
ANNALY MORTAGE MGMT Inc.	NLY	B	17.02	-10.18 / 22	18.18 / 69	1.88	11.32	1.93
TDC A/S -ADR	TLD	B-	16.89	20.45 / 50	2.50 / 43	0.71	10.98	1.85
ENERPLUS RESOURCES FUND	ERF	B	29.19	36.40 / 64	33.05 / 85	1.71	10.95	3.20
MCG CAPITAL CORP	MCGC	B-	15.14	5.00 / 33	———	1.04	10.92	1.65
CAPITAL ALLIANCE INCM TRUST	CAA	B	16.80	-5.06 / 25	18.30 / 69	1.36	10.77	1.81
DOMINION RES BLACK WARRIO	DOM	A	32.15	21.32 / 51	30.43 / 83	2.47	10.59	3.40
TV AZTECA SA DE CV -ADR	TZA	B-	8.37	29.22 / 58	15.22 / 64	0.26	10.55	0.88
COMPANIA CERVECERIA -ADR	CU	B	21.43	33.91 / 62	6.79 / 49	1.43	10.52	2.25
LL&E ROYALTY TRUST	LRT	B	4.92	93.29 / 85	18.00 / 69	0.51	10.40	0.51
BP PRUDHOE BAY ROYALTY TRT	BPT	A	35.27	112.18 / 88	48.58 / 92	2.66	10.39	3.67
HANOVER CAPITAL MTG HLDGS	HCM	B-	12.10	31.62 / 61	35.16 / 86	1.30	10.20	1.23
WILLIAMS COAL SEAM RYL TRT	WTU	B	15.81	49.52 / 72	15.19 / 64	1.56	10.07	1.59
AMERICAN CAPITAL STRGS	ACAS	A-	28.02	13.20 / 42	9.91 / 55	2.56	9.99	2.80
BRT REALTY TRUST	BRT	A-	19.50	21.23 / 51	37.13 / 87	2.03	9.85	1.92
RAIT INVESTMENT TRUST	RAS	A-	25.06	17.80 / 47	26.89 / 80	2.22	9.74	2.44
THORNBURG MORTGAGE Inc.	TMA	B	27.65	9.26 / 38	30.57 / 83	2.77	9.65	2.67
SANTA FE ENERGY TRUST	SFF	A	29.28	29.34 / 59	21.28 / 73	2.81	9.56	2.80
PMC COMMERCIAL TRUST	PCC	A-	14.19	17.62 / 47	9.53 / 54	1.21	9.44	1.34
SAN JUAN BASIN ROYALTY TR	SJT	A	24.95	68.11 / 79	32.70 / 85	1.96	9.42	2.35
ALLIED CAPITAL CP	ALD	B-	23.88	11.18 / 40	9.55 / 54	1.60	9.34	2.23
HELLENIC TELECOM ORG	OTE	B-	6.50	15.88 / 45	-0.55 / 38	0.56	9.08	0.59
TSR Inc.	TSRI	B-	6.65	-0.91 / 28	21.15 / 73	0.47	8.89	0.59
DORCHESTER MINERALS -LP	DMLP	B-	18.89	14.00 / 43	21.31 / 73	-0.84	8.74	1.65
VOLVO AB SWE -ADR	VOLVY	A	33.37	52.75 / 74	37.27 / 87	0.68	8.65	2.89
AMERIGAS PARTNERS -LP	APU	B	26.69	6.55 / 35	13.17 / 60	1.49	8.47	2.26
ARIZONA LAND INCOME -CL A	AZL	B-	4.68	18.76 / 48	18.05 / 69	0.56	8.42	0.39
PERMIAN BASIN ROYALTY TRST	PBT	A-	9.47	32.00 / 61	24.35 / 77	0.74	8.37	0.79
CROSS TIMBERS ROYALTY TRST	CRT	A	29.45	29.52 / 59	24.72 / 78	2.19	8.01	2.36
NORTHERN BORDER PARTNRS	NBP	B-	41.80	4.08 / 33	9.66 / 55	-2.03	8.01	3.35
HRPT PROPERTIES TRUST	HRP	B+	10.22	17.76 / 47	14.41 / 63	0.60	7.99	0.82
ENBRIDGE ENERGY PRTNRS	EEP	B	48.09	8.87 / 37	6.35 / 48	1.81	7.99	3.84
MESA ROYALTY TRUST	MTR	A-	59.95	28.96 / 58	17.70 / 68	5.02	7.93	4.76
GREAT NORTHERN IRON ORE	GNI	A+	99.00	35.33 / 64	21.93 / 74	6.98	7.91	7.83
NATIONAL HEALTH REALTY Inc.	NHR	A-	17.90	21.18 / 51	17.93 / 69	1.27	7.86	1.41
NATIONWIDE HEALTH PPTYS	NHP	B-	19.25	24.68 / 54	7.86 / 51	0.84	7.83	1.51

Table 3: High-Dividend Yielding Stocks (continued)

Company Name	Stock Ticker Symbol	Overall Weiss Investment Rating	Stock Price as of 07/16/04	1-Year Total Return (%) / Percentile	3-Year Total Return (%) / Percentile	Earnings per Share $	Div. Yield	Div. Rate
ENERGY TRANSFER PARTNERS	ETP	B-	39.78	36.65 / 65	23.00 / 76	3.59	7.68	3.06
AGREE REALTY CORP	ADC	B	25.18	13.62 / 42	17.67 / 68	1.87	7.67	1.93
HUGOTON ROYALTY TRUST	HGT	A	23.53	48.12 / 72	33.40 / 85	2.06	7.57	1.78
MONMOUTH RE INVEST CP	MNRTA	B-	7.77	1.51 / 30	15.60 / 65	0.55	7.45	0.58
COMML NET LEASE RLTY Inc.	NNN	A-	17.40	3.05 / 32	16.22 / 66	1.15	7.44	1.29
GULFTERRA ENERGY PARTNERS	GTM	A	39.90	9.41 / 38	7.02 / 50	1.48	7.44	2.97
HEALTH CARE REIT Inc.	HCN	B	33.00	13.15 / 42	17.03 / 67	1.43	7.39	2.44
SENIOR HOUSING PPTYS TRUST	SNH	B	17.30	34.15 / 63	18.75 / 70	0.81	7.39	1.28
KANEB PIPELINE PARTNRS -LP	KPP	B+	47.50	10.61 / 39	13.44 / 61	2.56	7.32	3.48
EASTERN AMERN NATURAL GAS	NGT	A-	23.70	17.95 / 47	15.84 / 65	1.89	7.32	1.73
SABINE ROYALTY TRUST	SBR	A	35.54	47.55 / 71	22.23 / 75	2.62	7.28	2.59
ONE LIBERTY PROPERTIES Inc.	OLP	B	18.19	5.86 / 34	17.05 / 67	1.10	7.27	1.32

Data date 07/16/04. For the most recent version of this list, please visit www.WeissRatings.com, go to "Products" and click on "Stocks."

But what if Kathleen changes her mind later and wants to take on more risk? What would her best choices be? If Kathleen has time to ride out the waves in the market, then she may want to consider more aggressive growth stocks. The following list is a sample of the top 25 aggressive growth stocks.

Table 4: Aggressive Growth Stocks

(See Appendix E for a description of each column.)

Company Name	Stock Ticker Symbol	Overall Weiss Investment Rating	Stock Price as of 07/16/04	1-Year Total Return (%) / Percentile	3-Year Total Return (%) / Percentile	Earnings per Share $
AAMES FINANCIAL CORP.	AMSF	C	3.00	7.41 / 36	35.72 / 86	9.07
ALLIANCE RESOURCE PTNRS -LP	ARLP	B-	47.89	78.86 / 83	35.15 / 86	2.91
AMERICAN HOME MTG INVT CORP	AHM	C	26.01	43.21 / 69	20.70 / 72	3.97
CERAMICS PROCESS SYSTEMS CP	CPSX	C-	0.73	112.50 / 88	33.16 / 85	0.02
CTI INDUSTRIES CORP	CTIB	C	2.72	22.22 / 52	13.21 / 61	0.25
CYBERONICS Inc.	CYBX	C	29.31	8.21 / 37	21.17 / 73	0.29
IMPAC MORTGAGE HLDGS Inc.	IMH	C	21.63	66.53 / 79	66.99 / 95	2.73
INDYMAC BANCORP Inc.	NDE	C	30.96	26.84 / 56	5.52 / 47	3.10
INFODATA SYSTEMS Inc.	INFD	C-	1.63	187.50 / 94	23.73 / 77	0.08
ITEX CORP	ITEX	C	0.22	70.59 / 80	8.03 / 51	0.08
KANEB SERVICES LLC	KSL	C	29.80	5.03 / 34	30.84 / 83	1.93
MAMMA.COM Inc.	MAMA	C-	8.36	175.86 / 93	58.74 / 94	0.12
NEW CENTURY FINANCIAL CORP	NCEN	C	43.55	86.78 / 84	95.06 / 98	8.58
NEW ENGLAND REALTY ASSC -LP	NEN	C-	66.50	25.22 / 55	34.66 / 86	10.85
ORIX CORP -ADR	IX	C-	54.41	77.88 / 82	3.08 / 44	3.06
REDWOOD TRUST Inc.	RWT	C-	54.72	55.32 / 75	46.06 / 91	9.11
ROBOCOM SYSTEMS INTL Inc.	RIMS	C-	0.69	42.22 / 69	74.72 / 96	0.14
ROCKWELL MED TECHNOLOGIES	RMTI	C-	2.72	19.55 / 49	38.03 / 88	0.02
SILVERSTAR HOLDINGS LTD	SSTR	C-	0.93	27.54 / 57	5.47 / 47	0.14
STRATFORD AMERICAN CORP	STFA	C-	0.41	50.00 / 73	23.31 / 76	0.06

Table 4: Aggressive Growth Stocks (continued)

Company Name	Stock Ticker Symbol	Overall Weiss Investment Rating	Stock Price as of 07/16/04	1-Year Total Return (%) / Percentile	3-Year Total Return (%) / Percentile	Earnings per Share $
TOWN & COUNTRY TRUST	TCT	C-	25.12	12.33 / 41	14.60 / 63	0.64
TUNEX INTERNATIONAL Inc.	TNEX	C-	0.55	37.50 / 65	0.61 / 40	0.04
USG CORP	USG	C	18.01	30.30 / 59	50.11 / 92	3.19
VENTAS Inc.	VTR	C	24.20	58.58 / 76	33.67 / 85	1.04
W HOLDING CO Inc.	WHI	C	17.21	43.02 / 69	36.21 / 87	1.09

Data date 07/16/04. For the most recent version of this list, please visit www.WeissRatings.com, go to "Products" and click on "Stocks."

In addition, she may want to look at stocks from a few sectors, such as energy, financials, healthcare, telecommunication services, or utilities to diversify and balance her risk.

Table 5: Top-Performing Stocks by Sector

(See Appendix E for a description of each column.)

**EN = Energy; FN = Financials; HC = Health
TS = Telecommunication Services; UT = Utilities**

Company Name	Industry/ Sector Code	Stock Ticker Symbol	Overall Weiss Investment Rating	Stock Price as of 07/16/04	1-Year Total Return (%) / Percentile	3-Year Total Return (%) / Percentile	Earnings per Share $
CONOCOPHILLIPS	EN	COP	A+	77.35	50.38 / 73	12.43 / 59	7.23
MURPHY OIL CORP	EN	MUR	A+	78.05	59.58 / 77	24.92 / 78	3.14
PATINA OIL & GAS CORP	EN	POG	A+	30.74	114.71 / 88	59.69 / 94	1.60
TEEKAY SHIPPING CORP	EN	TK	A+	38.06	75.71 / 82	32.78 / 85	3.87
XTO ENERGY Inc.	EN	XTO	A+	30.91	102.42 / 87	52.21 / 93	1.37
BROWN & BROWN Inc.	FN	BRO	A+	43.15	39.90 / 67	23.87 / 77	1.70
DELPHI FINANCIAL GRP -CL A	FN	DFG	A+	43.60	31.15 / 60	22.55 / 75	3.17
SELECTIVE INS GROUP Inc.	FN	SIGI	A+	39.45	60.64 / 77	16.40 / 66	2.54
STATE AUTO FINL CORP	FN	STFC	A+	30.16	34.79 / 63	24.40 / 77	1.62
ZENITH NATIONAL INS	FN	ZNT	A+	50.67	97.50 / 86	23.92 / 77	3.50
BARD (C.R.) Inc.	HC	BCR	A+	54.73	59.44 / 77	25.63 / 78	1.87
COOPER COMPANIES Inc.	HC	COO	A+	59.13	72.94 / 81	29.73 / 82	2.50
DENTSPLY INTERNATL Inc.	HC	XRAY	A+	51.67	21.63 / 51	20.83 / 73	2.16
MESA LABORATORIES Inc.	HC	MLAB	A+	10.00	37.18 / 65	30.57 / 83	0.70
MINE SAFETY APPLIANCES CO	HC	MSA	A+	32.32	128.05 / 90	48.06 / 92	1.48
ATLANTIC TELE-NETWORK Inc.	TS	ANK	A+	32.00	43.93 / 70	36.39 / 87	2.51
MOBILE TELESYSTEMS OJS	TS	MBT	A-	114.47	109.37 / 87	65.47 / 95	5.22
NORTH PITTSBURGH SYSTMS	TS	NPSI	A	18.60	6.42 / 35	17.41 / 68	1.03
PERUSAHAAN INDO SAT	TS	IIT	B+	24.13	142.42 / 91	35.89 / 87	2.35
CONSOLIDATED WATER CO	UT	CWCO	A+	25.31	77.58 / 82	36.25 / 87	0.96
ENERGEN CORP	UT	EGN	A	47.71	45.81 / 71	24.00 / 77	3.28
ENERGYSOUTH Inc.	UT	ENSI	A+	39.76	31.44 / 60	27.03 / 80	2.46
NEW JERSEY RESOURCES	UT	NJR	A	41.50	21.95 / 52	15.80 / 65	2.78
QUESTAR CORP	UT	STR	A+	38.95	23.43 / 53	21.10 / 73	2.22

Data date 07/16/04. For the most recent version of this list, please visit www.WeissRatings.com, go to "Products" and click on "Stocks."

Kathleen sits back with a big sigh of relief. She's go
options. Risk isn't so scary once you understand it
to benefit from it. She's not lost in the investing ju

Chapter 10

Slim Down (On Debt) and Gain (Financial) Muscle

I n the midst of our discussion about investing, we'd like to say a word — or four! — about debt: **GET — RID — OF — IT!**

Carrying high credit-card and consumer debt, while thinking and dreaming about investing in the stock market, is like walking into the jungle with a heavy pack on your back. Eventually, that weight on your back is going to wear you out and force you to quit.

According to the Federal Reserve, the average U.S. household credit card debt is now more than $6,500. Well, you say, I'm not that bad — I'm only carrying about $2,500. Not bad? Really? If you're paying 18% interest on credit card debt, that means you're paying $38 a month in interest payments. In other words — you're investing in debt when you could be investing in your future! What if you saved that money instead and invested it in the stock market?

Years	Earnings of $38 invested per month earning 8%
5	$2,792
10	$6,951
15	$13,149

Wow is right. At the end of five years, you've saved $2,792. After 10 years, you've hit $6,951. And in 15 years, you've hit

$13,149. You probably haven't thought of it this way, but you've really been investing in debt instead of investing in yourself!

But, you say, I can't save! We understand; it's not easy.

You say you don't have $1,000 to start with? You do, it's right in your pocket, those hidden dollars that slip through your fingers every day. You can save $4 a day, 250 days a year. Bring your lunch to work, skip the lattes, cut down on soda pop, and walk a few more blocks to your bank's ATM to save the fee. You'll be surprised how quickly that hidden money can add up.

Invest that $1,000 each year at 5%, and what happens? It grows to an amazing $72,247 by the time you reach 65 (assuming you started investing at 35).

Push yourself a little bit more, and you'll be surprised at what happens:

Without too much trouble, you can double your savings to $166 a month, by trimming down on some overlooked costs. That adds up to $2,000 a year.

Finding Money to Save

Tip	Monthly Savings
Save .50 a day in loose change	$15
Cut soda/pop consumption by 1 liter a week	$6
At work, substitute one coffee for one cappuccino	$40
Bring lunch to work (saving estimated $3/day)	$60
Eat out two fewer times a month	$30
Borrow, rather than buy, one book a month	$15
Comparison shop for gas (save est. $.25/gallon)	$4
Maintain checking account minimum to avoid fees	$7
Bounce one less check a month	$20
Pay credit card bill on time to avoid late fee	$25
Pay off $1,000 of credit card debt, reducing interest	$15

Source: AmericaSaves

The Miracle of Compounding

Start investing that money each month when you're 25, at 5% in the stock market, a very conservative rate, and what happens? It grows to $253,319 by the time you reach 65!

Double your rate of return to 10%, and yes, you're speechless. A whopping $1,049,797! But we (hate to say it!) knew it all along.

How did this happen? It's called the miracle of **compounding**. Even Einstein, who called the law of gravity the first miracle, called compounding a miracle.

How does compounding work? It's simple. You make money when the interest you earn also earns interest. In other words, you earn money, not only on your original investment, but also on the money that you earned since you started investing. For example, if you start with $100 and earn 10%, at the end of the first year you have $110. If you earn another 10% the second year, that's 10% of $110, which is $121. Notice that, at the start of the second year, you had a bigger base ($110) to invest. And as a result, you make $11 in the second year, a little bit more than in the first year. For the third year, it would be 10% of $121, which brings you to $133.10, earnings of $12.10 a little more than the second year ... and so on. The longer you invest your money, the more compounding works for you.

To take advantage of compounding with stock investing, choose dividend-paying stocks that automatically reinvest the dividends you earn. Tell your broker to use the dividends they pay you to buy more of that stock. That's an excellent way to grow your investment quickly.

Take a closer look at how compounding works with the graphic on the next page ...

Stocks providing high-dividend yields have traditionally been a favorite investment for investors in or approaching retirement. In addition to providing a regular stream of income, dividends offer a cushion to investors in bear markets and a source of stability during bull markets. The stock history books show that dividend-paying stocks tend to outperform non-dividend-paying stocks, especially in bear markets. Now with the change in tax treatment

The Miracle of Compound Interest

Watch Your Savings Grow

**Save $50 a Month
With a 5% Yield**

Few people get rich from their wages alone. But by taking advantage of the "miracle" of compound interest — earning interest on your interest — almost anyone can reach long-term financial goals.

By saving as little as $50 a month, you can build considerable savings. The chart tells the story.

| 1 Year $614 | 5 Years $3,400 | 10 Years $7,764 | 25 Years $29,775 | 40 Years $76,301 |

Source: AmericaSaves

for dividend payments, these stocks are becoming increasingly attractive for all investors, not just retirees.

Start Saving the Smart Way — With Tax-Free Dollars!

Choose to save your money in tax-deductible plans or accounts whenever possible; contributions to these plans are generally tax-deductible on both the federal and state level. In addition, on the back end, they give you the added benefit of sheltering your money from tax once you invest. Now for a brief tour of the choices:

A Little Help From Uncle Sam

Company-Based Plans

If you work for a for-profit company with a 401(k) plan, you can save up to $13,000 (for tax year 2004). This limit is scheduled to grow by $1,000 per year until it reaches $15,000 in 2006. Nonprofit organizations offer its cousin, a 403(b) plan. Employees with these plans can contribute up to $13,000. In addition to the tax savings, employers often match your contribution. If you're self-employed, a SEP-IRA (Simplified Employee Pension Individual Retirement Account) allows you to save $40,000, or 25% of your self-employment income. **Keogh** plans are a second choice, allowing $30,000 annually, or 15%.

IRA Accounts

If your company doesn't offer a retirement savings plan, or you've maxxed out your contribution at work, you can save in an Individual Retirement Account (IRA). The maximum annual contribution limit for a traditional IRA is $3,000 for 2003 and $3,500 for 2003 if you are 50 or older. You may or may not be able to deduct your full IRA contribution if you have a company plan. If you can't deduct your contribution to an IRA, then consider a Roth IRA (or IRA Plus). The "plus" is for the fact that, although your contribution isn't tax deductible, you don't pay tax on whatever you earn inside the account, or income tax on qualified withdrawals. For more information on IRAs, go to www.irs.gov. To open an IRA, you may want to seek the advice of a broker. To learn more about working with a broker, refer to Chapter 16.

Dollar-Cost Averaging Evens Out the Terrain

Because the stock market can be affected by so many different indicators and issues, it's vulnerable to daily ups and downs. That's why trying to "time the market" is not a wise investment strategy.

Dollar-cost averaging is a way for you to profit from the downs and minimize purchasing at the stock's highest purchase price. Let us explain. If you dollar-cost average on a weekly, monthly, or quarterly basis, you spend the same amount of money each interval to buy stock in that company. Some weeks, the price may be high — some weeks the price may be low. But over time, you will have bought the shares at an average price to maximize your returns without attempting to time the market. It will be your discipline that pays off, not your luck.

How it works: Dollar-cost averaging works because you're investing continuously and regularly. It's a great strategy to use, because it reduces your risk. Together with a portfolio that has broad diversification, you're building a solid investing foundation. Dollar-cost averaging won't automatically reap you a profit, but by sticking with it, you'll do better than investors who buy at market highs and sell at the lows.

Let's say you invest $100 every month in a stock trading initially at $50 a share. The first month, you buy two shares. Next month, if the stock moves up, to say, $100, you buy one share. But if the market drops, and the share price falls to $25, you get four shares. Over time, if you're disciplined and keep investing on a regular schedule, that means you ride out the ups and downs of the market easily because the ups — getting to buy more shares when the price is low — will even out the downs — buying less when the price is high.

So by this point, you've got debt out of the picture, or under control, and you're saving regularly. But you haven't started to invest, because you're thinking — I don't have enough to invest in the stock market.

You've got two choices to tap:

Start slowly, with a DRIP or a DIP. Whaaat? Dividend Reinvestment Plans and Direct Investment Plans can help you out here. If you have only $25 or $50 a month to invest in the stock market, you don't want to pay commissions to a broker. This is your best strategy. More and more companies are selling their stock directly through DRIPs, which give you the opportunity to invest cash and/or automatically reinvest dividends, to buy more shares. For more information, check The Moneypaper (www.moneypaper.com). Hundreds of companies also offer DIPs, with investment minimums as low as $250 (Exxon Mobil, Fannie Mae, and Home Depot, for instance) and $100, or even less (CVS). Go to Netstock Direct (www.netstockdirect.com) for a complete list of companies. Both plans share the same good features: low minimum investment, no broker's fee, and automatic reinvestment of dividends, with the option to receive a cash dividend. So you get the double whammy of both dollar-cost averaging and compounding at the same time!

Another round of congratulations is in order! You've faced a few lions in the investing jungle, and you're still standing. Part III is coming up, with a step-by-step explanation of how to understand a stock's performance. We're getting close to the end of the trail ...

Part III

Know the Trail

- Identifying Quality Stocks
- Selecting a Broker
- Monitoring Your Investments

Chapter 11

Where Do I Look for the Right Clues?

Remember the words of wisdom that our Wise Guide provided to Kathleen and the map that he helped her create in Part II? Well, now it's time for our Wise Guide to show Kathleen how to research and understand stock performance so she'll be able to choose the best trail (given her personal risk zone) to reach her financial dreams.

Back home, a friend of Kathleen's told her that it's a good idea to buy stock in companies that you know. Well, Kathleen knows Coca-Cola Co. — she certainly enjoys drinking it. She wonders: would Coca-Cola Co. be worth buying? And can she afford it? It's so popular, and it's been on the market for years. So that's all she needs to know — the price, right?

Price is important — but it isn't the only clue you study. Price by itself, or even in comparison to its sector or market index, doesn't give you the whole picture in terms of whether it's a good buy. A $100 stock can be underpriced, and a $15 stock can be overpriced. So, not only do you need to compare Coca-Cola Co.'s price to other stock prices, but you need to look for other clues.

In this book, we're going to demystify *all* of the clues you'll need to look at before you buy a stock. To help you research a stock, refer to the worksheet on page 77, which lists important factors to consider when analyzing a stock.

For purposes of our discussion, let's consider the stock of a fictional company, Kayaks R Us. Let's assume that the Weiss Investment Rating on Kayaks R Us is an A-, which means that the stock has a good track record of delivering a balance of performance and risk and that it is a good value with good prospects for outperforming the market. (To find the Weiss Investment Rating on stocks that you are considering, look for *Weiss Ratings' Ultimate Guided Tour of Stock Investing* in the reference section of many public libraries. The quarterly guide lists ratings on more than 6,000 stocks, including all those traded on the New York Stock Exchange, the American Stock Exchange and Nasdaq.) To purchase a stock rating, visit **www.WeissRatings.com** or call **1-800-289-9222**.

Now, let's go to **www.MartinWeiss.com,** where you can find a useful summary of information about any stock, as well as two big clues.

Go to the "Charts & Tools" tab on the top menu bar, then click on "Stock Quotes/Data Overview." Enter the company's ticker symbol, and a quick summary of important information about the stock will pop up. There's no need to be nervous — this is not unfamiliar territory. You've seen this information before in Part I: the exchange that the stock trades on, the stock's 52-week

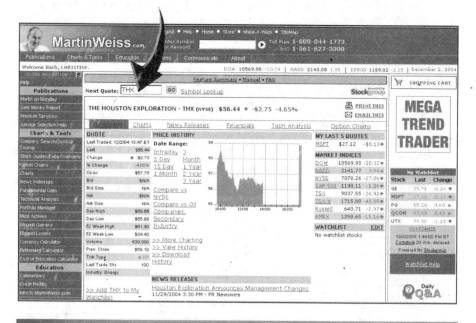

high and low prices, the stock's percent change, up or down, the shares outstanding, and the company's market capitalization.

But ... there are two new and mysterious terms, called "P/E" and "Earnings Per Share." P/E and EPS are so important in buying good stocks that we're going to stop and talk about them for a few minutes, so gather round:

"P/E" or Price-to-Earnings Ratio

This important clue gives you some of a stock's history over the past year, which is key. This clue tells you what investors really think of a stock's value; in other words, what price they are willing to pay for the per-share earnings of a company. If investors are willing to pay ten times earnings for one stock, as compared to paying five times earnings for another, you are right to assume that they think the first stock is viewed as more valuable.

A high P/E means investors have high expectations for future growth, which is a good thing, and have bid up the stock's price in anticipation. But stocks with very high P/Es may also be a very big gamble. Why? Because very high P/Es could be an indication that investors are paying too much for the stock and the price will start declining, or correcting, soon. Before you buy, it's also important to compare a stock's P/E to other stocks within the same industry to get a feel for whether the stock might be overvalued or undervalued. We'll show you how after we review another important clue.

Earnings Per Share, or EPS

This integral clue tells you how much a company really earns (in other words, its net income), divided by the number of outstanding shares, and after subtracting enough for taxes and preferred-stock dividends.

EPS helps you find companies with a good record of rising earnings. This is how much the company earned per share in the most recent four quarters. For example, in March 2004, the per-share earnings of the company are estimated based on the period from April 2003 to March 2004. If it's September 2004, this would be the per-share earnings from October 2003 to September 2004 ... you're getting the idea.

Now, it's time to get out the map — we're ready to make some serious progress on the trail. Throughout the next few chapters, we'll walk you through each line of the worksheet and help you build your analysis. We'll use Kayaks R Us as an example. If you want to research an actual stock online, you'll also find the worksheet information at **www.MartinWeiss.com**. From the top menu go to "MyMenu" and then click on "My Stock Comparison Worksheet."

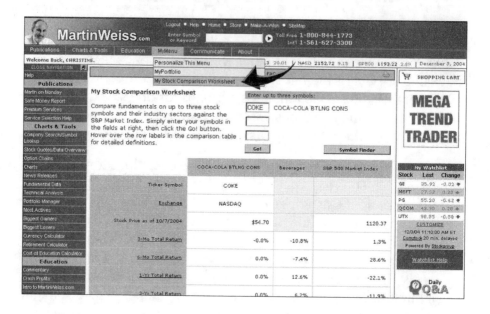

Line 1 – Ticker. Each stock has a "ticker" symbol, which identifies it. This is the first clue you look for and the most basic one. If you didn't know a stock's ticker symbol, you could enter the wrong company's name and buy stock in an entirely different company. For example, if you incorrectly entered the name of our fictional company, Kayaks R Us, you could very easily pull up information about Kayaks Rus, a completely different company. Naturally, this is only an example, but in the real world, there are many companies with similar names. Be sure to use the correct ticker symbol!

What's another good clue to look for to be sure that you've got the right company? The size of the company, or its market

Stock Comparison Worksheet

	Stock 1	Stock 2	Stock 3	Industry	Market Index
1. Ticker					
2. Weiss Invstmnt Rating					
3. Exchange					
4. Stock Price					
5. 3-Mo. Total Return					
6. 6-Mo. Total Return					
7. 1-Yr. Total Return					
8. 3-Yr. Total Return					
9. Earnings Per Share (EPS)					
10. Book Value Per Share					
11. Sales Per Share					
12. Price to Earnings (P/E)					
13. Price to Book Value (P/B)					
14. Price to Sales (P/S)					
15. 1-Yr. EPS Growth					
16. Dividend Per Share					
17. Dividend Yield					

capitalization. Companies fall into different market capitalization groupings, often defined as follows:

- ▲ Micro – $250 million or less
- ▲ Small – $250 million to $1 billion
- ▲ Mid – $1 billion to $5 billion
- ▲ Large – $5 billion or more

Line 2 – Weiss Investment Rating. You'll find samples of Weiss Investment Ratings in the back of this book. Our ratings allow you to instantly separate those stocks that have performed well and appear to represent a good value from those that are most likely to deliver weak future performance — but they're based on more than performance. We base our opinion on a broad range of information and analysis that also includes the various types of risk in the stock market. (See Appendix D for a description of our ratings.) Other firms that issue ratings often downplay investment risk and seldom, if ever, issue negative ratings. No one can guarantee a stock's future performance, but our analysis provides a solid framework for making informed investment decisions. Use this information, along with other factors related to your own personal financial situation, when you make a decision to buy or sell a stock. (Remember, you can find Weiss Investment Ratings on more than 6,000 stocks by referencing *Weiss Ratings' Ultimate Guided Tour of Stock Investing,* which can be found at many public libraries.) You can also purchase a stock rating at **www.WeissRatings.com** or call **1-800-289-9222**.

Line 3 – Exchange. The exchange is the place where shares of stock are bought and sold, as we discussed in Part I. Knowing the exchange that a stock is traded on will help you locate it in your local newspaper stock listings. The New York Stock Exchange on Wall Street is the largest. There's also the American Stock Exchange, with locations in Boston, Philadelphia, Chicago, Cincinnati, and San Francisco, and the NASDAQ, or National Association of Securities Dealers Automated Quotation System.

Line 4 – Stock Price. This is the price you pay to own a share of stock. You can find the price by checking the stock listings in a newspaper, the company's website, or the exchanges. Let's suppose Kayaks R Us' stock price is $51.26.

So far, so good. Now we're ready to look at one of the most important clues in picking a good stock.

Chapter 12

It's All About Performance

Now you've got to dig into the barrel a little more and sort through the apples available for sale. What determines a good pick or a bad one? A key clue is performance. It measures the return on your investment. It's simple to understand.

Every investor, of course, would like to know a stock's return on an investment in advance. You can't — no one can! Past performance, which can be influenced by several factors over periods of time, is a key clue. Those factors include major events affecting a company, sales, net income, and earnings growth, and perceived value of the stock. By studying performance over time, you get a good picture of how a stock has done.

Price Increases

\- Price Declines

\+ Current Income (dividends)

_____

= RETURN

Back to the worksheet …

Line 5 – 3-Month Total Return. Many stocks can perform well in a very short period of time. Check this number and then:

Line 6 – 6-Month Total Return. Look again. How has the stock performed over a little bit more time? But don't stop there:

Line 7 – 1-Year Total Return. Heard the phrase, "flash in the pan?" Don't pick a stock that dazzles investors for a season. Keep looking:

Line 8 – 3-Year Total Return. Now you've arrived — three years is a good indicator of how a stock is performing.

If current income is a priority and you're interested in dividend-paying stocks, review the sample of high-rated stocks with the highest dividend yields listed on pages 58.

Kathleen is beginning to realize that on this safari into the world of stock investing, there are lots of clues to help you reach your destination. So she looks at the next clues carefully which are discussed in Chapter 13.

Survival Tip
Future Performance

Keep in mind that past performance alone isn't always a true indicator of the future. Stocks may have already experienced a run-up in price and could be due for a correction. Also remember: In a market downturn, the stocks with the greatest previous gains will often be among the stocks with the greatest future losses.

Show Me the MONEY!

There's one question every investor wants to know: How much is the company earning? The next clue on the worksheet answers that question. Here's how:

Line 9 – Earnings Per Share (EPS). We talked about this clue earlier, but it's so important, we'll repeat the information. EPS is how much money the company is earning, divided by the total number of shares outstanding. In other words, how much profit per share of stock is the company making. "Shares outstanding" are simply the number of shares of stock a company has circulating in the marketplace.

You'll use the EPS to find companies with a good earnings outlook. For example, Kayaks R Us recently reported EPS of $0.65 for the second quarter of 2004.

Where will you find EPS? Often, you'll hear newscasters talking about earnings per share of a particular company on the evening news. Another source of information: the company itself, which issues quarterly earnings reports. The **10-Q** and **10-K** reports of a publicly traded company have this information. You can also find information about a particular stock on the website of the company, one of the stock exchanges, **www.MartinWeiss.com**, or by contacting the Securities and Exchange Commission, which monitors the industry (www.sec.gov).

But in studying a stock's value, it's smart to look at more than one statistic. Other measures include the per-share values of a company's "book value," or net worth, and its sales.

Line 10 – Book Value Per Share is a company's assets minus its liabilities (what it owns minus what it owes) divided by the number of shares outstanding. In other words, the portion of the company's equity, or net worth, that is allocated to each share of stock. Let's assume Kayaks R Us' book value per share is $6.03 as of the second quarter 2004.

By checking back on **www.MartinWeiss.com**, you can find the book value per share of the stock that you're interested in researching. If you want to crunch the numbers yourself, you'll find a company's equity on the balance sheet of the financial statement.

Now we're ready for:

Line 11 – Sales Per Share. This tells you how much money the company took in, or how much money it earned from selling its products or services, divided by the number of shares outstanding. In other words, the portion of the company's sales allocated to each outstanding share of stock.

Kayaks R Us' sales per share value was $9.00. To crunch the numbers yourself, you'll find sales activity on the income statement of the financial statement.

To recap, you now know how much of the company's profits, net worth, and sales are assigned to each share of stock. What does that mean? Well, the meaning lies in the comparison of those figures to the price of the stock. So let's go on to discuss what are known as valuation ratios.

Let's look again at the Price-to-Earnings, or P/E, ratio.

Chapter 14

It's the Price That Counts

Before you buy, it's important to check a stock's P/E to make sure you're not paying too much. You compare a stock's P/E to stocks within the same industry to get a feel for whether the stock might be overpriced or underpriced compared to its peers, and to the average P/E of its market index.

Line 12 – Price to Earnings, or P/E, is a key clue because it measures a stock's value and tells you what investors really think of it, by how much they are willing to pay for it: too much, too little, or just enough.

It's simple to understand: If a stock's P/E is 12, that means you're willing to pay $12 for every dollar of earnings. For Kayaks R Us, the P/E is 25.6. The higher the ratio, the more investors are willing to pay for the company's earnings because they are expecting earnings to grow.

Say you have a choice of buying stock from two companies, Stock #1 sells at $50 a share, and Stock #2 at $100. You would logically think that you're getting a better deal with Stock #1 at $50, right? Not necessarily.

If Stock #1 sells for $50, and the company earns $2.50 a share, the stock's price is 20 times earnings.

If Stock #2 sells for $100, and its earnings per share are twice as much as the other company, or $5.00, the P/E is 20 times, too. So this comparison shows you that the stock with the higher price (Stock #2) may not be overvalued at all. In fact, that stock may be a very good value.

Another example:

Stock #1 still sells for $50 and earns $2.50 a share, with a P/E equal to 20. Now we compare this with

Stock #3 that sells for the same price, $50, and earns twice as much, or $5.00 a share, giving it a P/E of 10. Stock #3 is a better value, because it sells for the same price as Stock #1, but is earning much more. In other words, investors have not overpriced its earnings.

If investors are willing to pay a price that's 50 times earnings for one stock, as compared to five times earnings for another, you are right to assume that they think the first stock is more valuable. A high P/E means investors have high expectations for future growth, which is a good thing, and have bid up the stock's price in anticipation. But, stocks with very high P/Es may also be a very big gamble. Why? High P/Es are often an indication that investors have bid up the price too much. Any slight misstep could cause the company to miss the expected earnings and, thus, the price comes falling down when investors see that the company didn't meet their expectations. Stocks with low P/Es are less risky, because it's easier for a company to meet those lower growth expectations.

On the next page is a sample list of 50 stocks with the lowest P/Es. Refer to the Glossary for column explanations.

Tip: If you want to study EPS in more detail, look for **projected annual earnings per share**, an estimate of what the company, or the analysts who track the company, think the stock is going to earn next year. And **price-to-projected-earnings,** which reflects how much you would pay for a dollar of projected earnings. It's like P/E, but for next year, and it's another measure of a company's expected growth. (For projected annual earnings per share and price-to-projected earnings on a particular stock, refer to *Weiss Ratings' Guide to Common Stocks* at your local library.)

Table 6: Low P/E Stocks

(See Appendix E for a description of each column.)

Company Name	Stock Ticker Symbol	Overall Weiss Investment Rating	Stock Price as of 07/16/04	1-Year Total Return (%) / Percentile	3-Year Total Return (%) / Percentile	Earnings per Share $
FRONTLINE LTD	FRO	B+	39.60	300.08 / 96	69.55 / 96	2.68
WINMILL & CO Inc. -CL A	WNMLA	B+	4.30	93.66 / 85	35.72 / 87	3.20
ARCH CAPITAL GROUP LTD	ACGL	A-	40.31	18.45 / 48	31.90 / 84	3.37
HALLWOOD GROUP Inc.	HWG	A-	49.00	175.36 / 93	103.58 / 98	3.44
FIRST AMERICAN CORP/CA	FAF	A-	25.77	6.70 / 35	9.74 / 55	4.80
NOVAMERICAN STEEL Inc.	TONS	A-	24.47	201.25 / 94	66.57 / 95	5.22
STEWART INFORMATION SRVC	STC	B+	32.95	14.16 / 43	21.01 / 73	5.25
MAX RE CAPITAL LTD	MXRE	B+	19.09	29.51 / 59	8.65 / 52	5.61
ODYSSEY RE HOLDINGS CORP	ORH	A-	24.20	30.00 / 59	12.63 / 60	5.93
RENAISSANCERE HOLDINGS	RNR	A	53.65	28.28 / 58	31.22 / 84	5.99
MFC BANCORP LTD	MXBIF	B+	18.54	87.72 / 84	27.95 / 81	6.14
KB HOME	KBH	B+	64.96	12.68 / 41	32.45 / 84	6.24
PETROKAZAKHSTAN Inc.	PKZ	A-	28.40	131.57 / 90	70.56 / 96	6.32
FIDELITY NATIONAL FINL Inc.	FNF	A-	37.46	43.65 / 69	30.73 / 83	6.61
IPC HOLDINGS LTD	IPCR	A-	38.57	12.81 / 41	19.67 / 71	6.67
BEAZER HOMES USA Inc.	BZH	B+	92.40	17.85 / 47	13.73 / 62	6.80
MARITRANS Inc.	TUG	B+	15.25	0.56 / 30	21.87 / 74	6.94
MANATRON Inc.	MANA	B+	8.31	10.57 / 39	28.58 / 81	7.31
INVESTORS TITLE CO	ITIC	B+	30.81	10.88 / 39	22.50 / 75	7.45
NVR Inc.	NVR	A	470.90	15.89 / 45	43.64 / 90	7.78
COMMERCE GROUP Inc./MA	CGI	A+	49.70	35.52 / 64	12.60 / 60	7.95
AMERICAN SAFETY INS HLDG	ASI	B+	13.82	28.02 / 57	13.73 / 62	8.07
SANDERSON FARMS Inc.	SAFM	A+	49.11	159.94 / 92	76.97 / 96	8.23
DXP ENTERPRISES Inc.	DXPE	A-	4.43	119.51 / 89	47.58 / 91	8.40
DEVON ENERGY CORP	DVN	A-	69.40	45.63 / 70	12.44 / 59	8.45
VILLAGE SUPER MARKET	VLGEA	A-	33.46	35.28 / 64	21.99 / 74	8.48
D R HORTON Inc.	DHI	B+	25.87	37.97 / 66	37.02 / 87	8.56
LENNAR CORP	LEN	B+	42.64	25.56 / 55	32.23 / 84	8.59
OMI CORP	OMM	A-	13.07	101.75 / 87	35.46 / 86	8.81
PETRO-CANADA	PCZ	A	44.95	14.26 / 43	23.12 / 76	8.91
NATL WSTN LIFE INS CO	NWLIA	B+	157.96	26.49 / 56	11.33 / 58	8.96
COMMERCIAL METALS	CMC	B+	34.00	85.27 / 84	28.14 / 81	9.01
PERUSAHAAN INDO SAT -ADR	IIT	B+	24.13	142.42 / 91	35.89 / 87	9.02
KNIGHTSBRIDGE TANKERS	VLCCF	B+	32.66	321.06 / 97	41.95 / 90	9.02
STIFEL FINANCIAL CORP	SF	A-	27.30	121.22 / 89	31.50 / 84	9.04
OLD REPUBLIC INTL CORP	ORI	A-	23.73	10.25 / 39	10.98 / 57	9.33
HAGGAR CORP	HGGR	A-	19.70	57.85 / 76	21.03 / 73	9.34
BERKLEY (W R) CORP	BER	A	42.77	33.04 / 62	35.34 / 86	9.37
SEMPRA ENERGY	SRE	A	34.50	28.59 / 58	13.14 / 60	9.41
ONEOK Inc.	OKE	B+	21.93	7.87 / 36	12.28 / 59	9.56
BRT REALTY TRUST	BRT	A-	19.50	21.23 / 51	37.13 / 87	9.61
TEEKAY SHIPPING CORP	TK	A+	38.06	75.71 / 82	32.78 / 85	9.67
PULTE HOMES Inc.	PHM	B+	50.06	60.43 / 77	38.75 / 88	9.67
EVEREST RE GROUP LTD	RE	A-	80.14	5.40 / 34	6.02 / 48	9.69
UNIVERSAL CORP/VA	UVV	B+	48.48	16.05 / 45	7.65 / 51	9.72
NATIONAL CITY CORP	NCC	A	34.85	7.78 / 36	7.15 / 50	9.78
CCA INDUSTRIES Inc.	CAW	A	10.25	25.27 / 55	86.09 / 97	9.81
BANCINSURANCE CORP	BCIS	A	7.90	44.93 / 70	17.00 / 67	9.81
CARVER BANCORP Inc.	CNY	B+	19.85	18.61 / 48	26.23 / 79	9.85
BALDWIN & LYONS	BWINA	A	25.88	15.74 / 45	12.42 / 59	9.87

Data date 07/16/04. For the most recent version of this list, please visit www.WeissRatings.com, go to "Products" and click on "Stocks."

Now let's look at Price to Book Value, or P/B.

Line 13 – Price to Book Value (P/B) is another measure of how expensive a stock is. It tells you how much investors are willing to pay for the company's net worth. The higher the ratio, the more they are willing to pay. It's calculated by dividing the stock price by the book value per share (discussed in prior chapter).

So the P/B for Kayaks R Us is 8.5.

Stock price	$51.26
Book value per share	$6.03
= Price to Book per share (P/B)	8.5

Let's move on to the next clue:

Line 14 – Price to Sales (P/S): Like P/E and P/B, **P/S** is another measure of a stock's valuation. It tells you how much investors are willing to pay for the company's revenues. The higher the ratio, the more they are willing to pay. It is calculated by dividing the stock price by the sales per share (discussed in prior chapter).

So the P/S for Kayaks R Us is 5.7.

Stock price	$51.26
Sales per share	$9.00
= Price to Sales per Share (P/S)	5.7

You did it! Congratulations! Now you can enjoy the next three clues, which are all about the money you earn when you invest in stock.

Line 15 – 1-Yr. EPS Growth Rate. Is the EPS rising or falling? The answer should be: It's rising! While nothing guarantees that a stock's price will rise, growing earnings is a must for any healthy company. It's an indication of a good investment that should make you money in the long run.

The one-year growth rate for Kayaks R Us' EPS is 20.6%. To determine whether this is good or bad, you could look up the growth rates of competitors of Kayaks R Us and compare the growth rates.

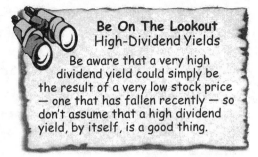

Be On The Lookout
High-Dividend Yields
Be aware that a very high dividend yield could simply be the result of a very low stock price — one that has fallen recently — so don't assume that a high dividend yield, by itself, is a good thing.

Line 16 – Dividend Per Share. As we discussed in Parts I and II, dividends are the portion of the company's current or past earnings that it distributes directly to shareholders. The dividend per share is the actual dollar amount that's paid out for each share. For example, if a company pays a dividend of $.50 per share and you own 100 shares, you will receive payment of $50 a year (usually divided into quarterly payments). Dividends are really only important to you if you want your investments to provide you with current income. If that's not your priority, then you only need to know the dividend rate for informational purposes.

The dividend per share for Kayaks R Us is $1.00. There is no formula for this — it's whatever the company decides the dividend will be.

Line 17 – Dividend Yield. The yield is the annual percentage rate of return paid in dividends on a share of stock. To figure out the dividend yield, divide the annual dividend by the current share price of a stock. Therefore, the dividend yield will fluctuate with the price of the stock.

For Kayaks R Us, the dividend yield is 2.0%.

Now where are we — are we at the end of the trail?

Sometimes, there isn't always a clear-cut answer. One company is not going to have it all: the lowest P/E, P/B, or P/S, with the best EPS growth rate and a high dividend yield. What's more likely is that it will become clear which companies look good, which look okay, and which ones don't look good at all.

Here's a sample list of stocks that have pulled it all together and performed consistently well with little risk.

Table 7: Top Performing Stocks With Low Risk
(See Appendix E for a description of each column.)

Company Name	Stock Ticker Symbol	Overall Weiss Investment Rating	Stock Price as of 07/16/04	1-Year Total Return (%) / Percentile	3-Year Total Return (%) / Percentile	Earnings per Share $
3M CO	MMM	A+	87.65	28.18 / 58	19.54 / 71	3.35
AARON RENTS Inc.	RNT	A+	32.51	72.09 / 81	40.60 / 89	1.12
AARON RENTS Inc.	RNT.A	A+	30.73	74.25 / 81	41.68 / 89	1.12
APPLIED SIGNAL TECHNOLOGY	APSG	A+	34.89	85.31 / 84	91.58 / 97	0.99
BHA GROUP HOLDINGS Inc.	BHAG	A+	37.85	75.32 / 82	34.77 / 86	1.87
BROWN & BROWN Inc.	BRO	A+	43.15	39.90 / 67	23.87 / 77	1.70
CANON Inc. -ADR	CAJ	A+	52.08	12.71 / 41	19.75 / 71	2.93
CHEROKEE Inc./DE	CHKE	A+	23.99	39.00 / 66	38.94 / 88	1.70
COHESANT TECHNOLOGIES Inc.	COHT	A+	12.59	268.32 / 96	76.41 / 96	0.65
CONOCOPHILLIPS	COP	A+	77.35	50.38 / 73	12.43 / 59	7.23
CONSOLIDATED WATER CO Inc.	CWCO	A+	25.31	77.58 / 82	36.25 / 87	0.96
COOPER COMPANIES Inc.	COO	A+	59.13	72.94 / 81	29.73 / 82	2.50
DENTSPLY INTERNATL Inc.	XRAY	A+	51.67	21.63 / 51	20.83 / 73	2.16
ENERGYSOUTH Inc.	ENSI	A+	39.76	31.44 / 60	27.03 / 80	2.46
ENNIS BUSINESS FORMS	EBF	A+	19.24	33.50 / 62	33.71 / 85	1.13
FEDEX CORP	FDX	A+	79.94	23.31 / 53	25.46 / 78	2.76
MARINE PRODUCTS CORP	MPX	A+	17.37	102.83 / 87	78.70 / 97	0.76
NOBILITY HOMES Inc.	NOBH	A+	21.24	128.20 / 90	30.71 / 83	0.93
PATINA OIL & GAS CORP	POG	A+	30.74	114.71 / 88	59.69 / 94	1.60
RAVEN INDUSTRIES Inc.	RAVN	A+	35.70	76.82 / 82	68.22 / 95	1.67
SANDERSON FARMS Inc.	SAFM	A+	49.11	159.94 / 92	76.97 / 96	4.52
SELECTIVE INS GROUP Inc.	SIGI	A+	39.45	60.64 / 77	16.40 / 66	2.54
TESMA INTERNATNAL Inc. -CL A	TSMA	A+	25.94	29.72 / 59	16.42 / 66	2.55
XTO ENERGY Inc.	XTO	A+	30.91	102.42 / 87	52.21 / 93	1.37
ZENITH NATIONAL INSURANCE CP	ZNT	A+	50.67	97.50 / 86	23.92 / 77	3.50

Data date 07/16/04. For the most recent version of this list, please visit www.WeissRatings.com, go to "Products" and click on "Stocks."

You'll have to decide which stock(s) to purchase, based on what's most important to you, your own personal financial situation and your risk tolerance.

How do you do that without losing your way?

Compare, Compare!

You've got a good grip on Kayaks R Us' value by understanding its price. Now you're ready to look at how Kayaks R Us' performance compares to competitors in its sector or industry, and finally, its market index.

When you go shopping, it's smart to compare what you want to buy, right? Same thing holds when shopping for stock.

Compare the stock that you're researching to competitors in its sector and within its industry. Also compare your stock to its market index. For example, we would compare Kayaks R Us to competitors in its sector (Consumer Discretionary) and within its industry (Specialty Retail), as well as the S&P 500.

If you want to find information about your stock and its competitors, here's what you can do …

Go back to **www.MartinWeiss.com**, and under "Charts & Tools" from the top menu bar, click on "Stock Quotes/Data Overview." Once there, type in the company name or symbol you are looking for. Since Kayaks R Us is not a real company, let's try putting in the symbol for Coca-Cola Co. Type 'COKE' into the Quote Lookup box and click "Go."

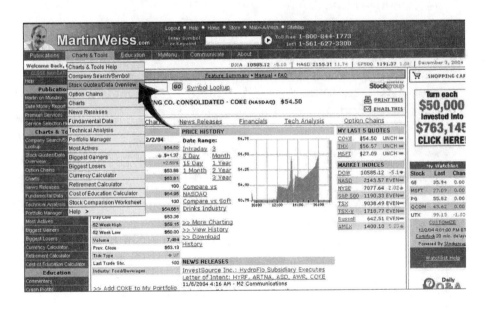

If you scroll down to the bottom of your screen , you'll see a list of Coca-Cola Co's top four competitors. Take a look at where your stock ranks in market "cap" — the current value of all of its stocks trading in the market.

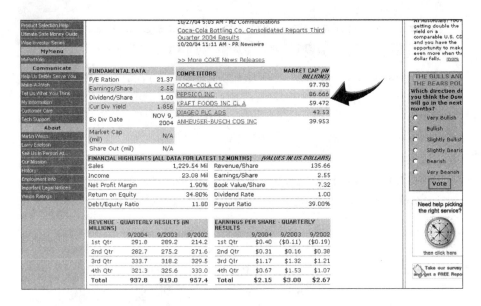

Click on the name of any of Coca Cola's competitors to view it's data overview page with comprehensive fundamentals and performance data. Want more?

Go to the "Charts &Tools" menu and click on "Charts." Again enter the symbol for Coca Cola (COKE) and view it's price performance graphically. See its performance vs. the Dow or enter 'PBG', the symbol for Pepsi in the "Compare vs Other Stocks" box and see how these two competitors match up.

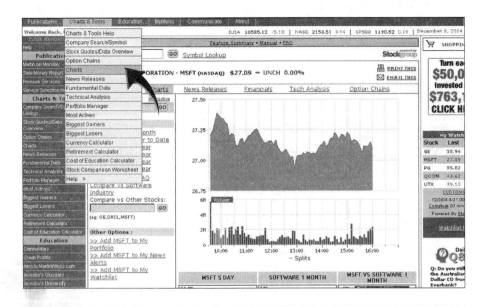

Here is a sample of stocks in each of the major indices that have outperformed their indices average results.

Table 8: Dow Jones Industrial Average Stocks That Have Outperformed the Index
[Market Index Return = 13.95%]

(See Appendix E for a description of each column.)

Company Name	Stock Ticker Symbol	Overall Weiss Investment Rating	Stock Price as of 07/16/04	1-Year Total Return (%) / Percentile	3-Year Total Return (%) / Percentile	1-Year Return Over Index Avg.
BOEING CO	BA	B	50.04	58.00 / 76	0.31 / 40	44.05
EXXON MOBIL CORP	XOM	A	45.45	31.99 / 61	5.96 / 48	18.04
ALTRIA GROUP Inc.	MO	B+	49.75	29.84 / 59	7.61 / 51	15.89
HONEYWELL INTERNATIONAL Inc.	HON	B	36.20	28.73 / 58	0.16 / 39	14.78
ALCOA Inc.	AA	B	32.42	28.47 / 58	-3.17 / 35	14.52
3M CO	MMM	A+	87.65	28.18 / 58	19.54 / 71	14.23
MCDONALDS CORP	MCD	B+	26.51	27.63 / 57	-3.75 / 35	13.68
GENERAL MOTORS CORP	GM	C	44.24	26.38 / 56	-3.97 / 35	12.43
PROCTER & GAMBLE CO	PG	A+	54.72	25.42 / 55	14.63 / 63	11.47
CATERPILLAR Inc.	CAT	B	77.08	21.58 / 51	16.63 / 67	7.63
UNITED TECHNOLOGIES CORP	UTX	A	89.76	19.81 / 49	8.11 / 52	5.86
DOW CHEMICAL	DOW	A-	39.15	19.76 / 49	8.23 / 52	5.81
GENERAL ELECTRIC CO	GE	B-	32.17	18.43 / 48	-5.98 / 32	4.47
DISNEY (WALT) CO	DIS	B	24.60	17.88 / 47	-1.32 / 38	3.93
COCA-COLA CO	KO	A-	51.02	15.82 / 45	2.56 / 43	1.87
AMERICAN EXPRESS	AXP	B+	50.01	14.14 / 43	11.06 / 57	0.19

Data date 07/16/04. For the most recent version of this list, please visit www.WeissRatings.com, go to "Products" and click on "Stocks."

Table 9: S&P 500 Stocks That Have Outperformed the Index
[Market Index Return = 12.95%]

(See Appendix E for a description of each column.)

Company Name	Stock Ticker Symbol	Overall Weiss Investment Rating	Stock Price as of 07/16/04	1-Year Total Return (%) / Percentile	3-Year Total Return (%) / Percentile	1-Year Return Over Index Avg.
AUTODESK Inc.	ADSK	A	39.17	158.68 / 92	27.45 / 80	145.73
ALLEGHENY TECHNOLOGIES Inc.	ATI	D	17.80	133.72 / 90	2.04 / 42	120.77
PENNEY (J C) CO	JCP	B	38.43	116.82 / 89	17.78 / 68	103.87
UNITED STATES STEEL CORP	X	C	34.38	115.91 / 88	20.52 / 72	102.96
ADVANCED MICRO DEVICES	AMD	C	14.81	113.88 / 88	1.83 / 42	100.93
VALERO ENERGY CORP	VLO	A	76.22	111.97 / 88	27.92 / 81	99.02
TXU CORP	TXU	B-	38.77	105.51 / 87	-1.36 / 37	92.56
COUNTRYWIDE FINANCIAL CORP	CFC	B-	69.90	101.12 / 86	47.15 / 91	88.17
ALLEGHENY ENERGY Inc.	AYE	D	14.92	100.27 / 86	-28.03 / 17	87.32
NORDSTROM Inc.	JWN	A+	41.61	99.22 / 86	29.86 / 82	86.27

Table 9: S&P 500 Stocks That Have Outperformed the Index [Market Index Return = 12.95%] (continued)

Company Name	Stock Ticker Symbol	Overall Weiss Investment Rating	Stock Price as of 07/16/04	1-Year Total Return (%) / Percentile	3-Year Total Return (%) / Percentile	1-Year Return Over Index Avg.
AVAYA Inc.	AV	C+	15.60	96.15 / 86	11.54 / 58	83.20
GOODYEAR TIRE & RUBBER CO	GT	D+	9.59	94.89 / 85	-26.48 / 18	81.94
MOTOROLA Inc.	MOT	B	17.50	94.44 / 85	0.01 / 39	81.49
ZIMMER HOLDINGS Inc.	ZMH	B+	85.21	94.11 / 85	49.23 / 92	81.16
RJ REYNOLDS TOBACCO HLDGS	RJR	C-	65.92	92.90 / 85	13.39 / 61	79.95
NOVELL Inc.	NOVL	C-	6.93	91.81 / 85	16.45 / 66	78.86
QUALCOMM Inc.	QCOM	B	70.56	90.99 / 85	4.23 / 45	78.04
PHELPS DODGE CORP	PD	C+	79.00	87.09 / 84	25.31 / 78	74.14
NATIONAL SEMICONDUCTOR CORP	NSM	B	19.62	86.52 / 84	7.43 / 50	73.57
LOUISIANA-PACIFIC CORP	LPX	B	22.09	85.52 / 84	28.11 / 81	72.57
BIOGEN IDEC Inc.	BIIB	C	61.51	82.53 / 83	2.76 / 43	69.58
SUNOCO Inc.	SUN	A-	66.69	82.04 / 83	26.01 / 79	69.09
YAHOO Inc.	YHOO	B	30.11	81.21 / 83	65.55 / 95	68.26
VISTEON CORP	VC	C	11.08	79.18 / 83	-11.63 / 27	66.23
ANDREW CORP	ANDW	C+	18.01	77.03 / 82	-4.06 / 35	64.08

Data date 07/16/04. For the most recent version of this list, please visit www.WeissRatings.com, go to "Products" and click on "Stocks."

Table 10: Wilshire 5000 Stocks That Have Outperformed the Index
[Market Index Return = 12.40%]

(See Appendix E for a description of each column.)

Company Name	Stock Ticker Symbol	Overall Weiss Investment Rating	Stock Price as of 07/16/04	1-Year Total Return (%) / Percentile	3-Year Total Return (%) / Percentile	1-Year Return Over Index Avg.
INSTEEL INDUSTRIES	IIIN	C	7.40	973.53 / 99	85.16 / 97	961.13
INDUSTRIAL SERVICES AMER Inc.	IDSA	C+	11.08	893.93 / 99	111.65 / 98	881.53
CEDARA SOFTWARE CORP	CDSWF	C	8.17	852.94 / 99	154.74 / 99	840.54
TITAN INTERNATIONAL Inc.	TWI	C	11.73	792.81 / 99	27.09 / 80	780.40
APTIMUS Inc.	APTM	C-	5.99	765.67 / 99	181.50 / 99	753.27
AIR T Inc.	AIRT	B+	18.89	543.29 / 98	63.42 / 95	530.89
NAVARRE CORP	NAVR	B	13.41	529.25 / 98	133.34 / 99	516.84
AUDIBLE Inc.	ADBL	D	12.38	522.73 / 98	109.03 / 98	510.33
RESEARCH IN MOTION	RIMM	B-	66.74	514.45 / 98	96.22 / 98	502.05
ACS-TECH80 LTD	ACSEF	B-	9.39	503.06 / 98	44.77 / 91	490.66
OMTOOL LTD	OMTL	D-	9.65	475.64 / 98	29.13 / 82	463.24
TRM CORP	TRMM	C	15.81	435.65 / 98	100.04 / 98	423.25
MARINER HEALTH CARE Inc.	MHCA	C-	26.51	435.64 / 98	————	423.24
ALDILA Inc.	ALDA	C	10.69	426.89 / 98	27.39 / 80	414.49
FIRST HORIZON PHARMACEUTICAL	FHRX	C	17.00	421.52 / 98	-9.63 / 29	409.12
SHILOH INDUSTRIES Inc.	SHLO	C+	16.04	419.11 / 98	32.80 / 85	406.71
OREGON STEEL MILLS Inc.	OS	C-	12.68	417.48 / 98	26.57 / 79	405.08
EVCI CAREER COLLEGES Inc.	EVCI	C+	10.21	409.85 / 98	122.47 / 99	397.45
SMTEK INTERNATIONAL Inc.	SMTI	C-	7.30	396.43 / 97	-6.12 / 32	384.03
DANIELSON HOLDING CORP	DHC	D	6.92	394.29 / 97	19.35 / 71	381.89

Table 10: Wilshire 5000 Stocks That Have Outperformed the Index
[Market Index Return = 12.40%] (continued)

Company Name	Stock Ticker Symbol	Overall Weiss Investment Rating	Stock Price as of 07/16/04	1-Year Total Return (%) / Percentile	3-Year Total Return (%) / Percentile	1-Year Return Over Index Avg.
TERRA INDUSTRIES Inc.	TRA	C	5.85	393.22 / 97	20.22 / 72	380.82
EFJ Inc.	EFJI	B	8.33	380.57 / 97	188.56 / 99	368.17
MANNING GREG AUCTIONS Inc.	GMAI	B	14.00	371.22 / 97	87.10 / 97	358.82
CAL-MAINE FOODS Inc.	CALM	B	14.09	365.47 / 97	93.69 / 98	353.07
BLUE COAT SYSTEMS Inc.	BCSI	D+	26.52	365.35 / 97	20.00 / 72	352.95

Data date 07/16/04. For the most recent version of this list, please visit www.WeissRatings.com, go to "Products" and click on "Stocks."

Table 11: Russell 2000 Stocks That Have Outperformed the Index
[Market Index Return = 19.53%]

(See Appendix E for a description of each column.)

Company Name	Stock Ticker Symbol	Overall Weiss Investment Rating	Stock Price as of 07/16/04	1-Year Total Return (%) / Percentile	3-Year Total Return (%) / Percentile	1-Year Return Over Index Avg.
NAVARRE CORP	NAVR	B	13.41	529.25 / 98	133.34 / 99	509.71
FIRST HORIZON PHARMACEUTICAL	FHRX	C	17.00	421.52 / 98	-9.63 / 29	401.99
OREGON STEEL MILLS Inc.	OS	C-	12.68	417.48 / 98	26.57 / 79	397.95
DANIELSON HOLDING CORP	DHC	D	6.92	394.29 / 97	19.35 / 71	374.76
TERRA INDUSTRIES Inc.	TRA	C	5.85	393.22 / 97	20.22 / 72	373.69
MANNING GREG AUCTIONS Inc.	GMAI	B	14.00	371.22 / 97	87.10 / 97	351.69
CAL-MAINE FOODS Inc.	CALM	B	14.09	365.47 / 97	93.69 / 98	345.94
BLUE COAT SYSTEMS Inc.	BCSI	D+	26.52	365.35 / 97	20.00 / 72	345.82
CARRIER ACCESS CORP	CACS	C	13.10	365.05 / 97	48.19 / 92	345.52
NOVATEL WIRELESS Inc.	NVTL	C	23.83	364.15 / 97	46.29 / 91	344.62
TRAVELZOO Inc.	TZOO	C	27.09	352.50 / 97	———	332.97
UROLOGIX Inc.	ULGX	C	13.44	330.82 / 97	0.14 / 39	311.29
MGP INGREDIENTS Inc.	MGPI	B	35.56	329.66 / 97	56.07 / 94	310.13
HANSEN NATURAL CORP	HANS	A	20.60	329.54 / 97	78.69 / 97	310.01
CHENIERE ENERGY Inc.	LNG	D	18.48	325.68 / 97	121.04 / 98	306.15
KERYX BIOPHARMACEUTICALS INC	KERX	D-	10.57	319.68 / 97	9.54 / 54	300.15
AMEDISYS INC	AMED	B+	27.02	317.05 / 97	73.38 / 96	297.52
MISSION RESOURCES CORP	MSSN	C	5.99	314.97 / 97	0.55 / 40	295.44
GIANT INDUSTRIES INC	GI	C+	22.41	297.90 / 96	40.23 / 89	278.37
NMS COMMUNICATIONS CORP	NMSS	D	6.76	296.18 / 96	27.66 / 80	276.65
DECKERS OUTDOOR CORP	DECK	A-	28.07	295.11 / 96	82.74 / 97	275.58
TESORO PETROLEUM CORP	TSO	B	28.90	275.46 / 96	35.50 / 86	255.93
BIOENVISION INC	BIV	D	7.73	269.05 / 96	63.44 / 95	249.52
DITECH COMMUNICATIONS CORP	DITC	C+	21.45	268.10 / 96	52.25 / 93	248.57
CALIFORNIA MICRO DEVICES CP	CAMD	C-	9.09	266.53 / 96	11.88 / 59	247.00

Data date 07/16/04. For the most recent version of this list, please visit www.WeissRatings.com, go to "Products" and click on "Stocks."

Table 12: NASDAQ Composite Stocks That Have Outperformed the Index

[Market Index Return = 11.91%]

(See Appendix E for a description of each column.)

Company Name	Stock Ticker Symbol	Overall Weiss Investment Rating	Stock Price as of 07/16/04	1-Year Total Return (%) / Percentile	3-Year Total Return (%) / Percentile	1-Year Return Over Index Avg.
INDUSTRIAL SERVICES AMER INC	IDSA	C+	11.08	893.93 / 99	111.65 / 98	882.02
AIR T INC	AIRT	B+	18.89	543.29 / 98	63.42 / 95	531.38
NAVARRE CORP	NAVR	B	13.41	529.25 / 98	133.34 / 99	517.34
RESEARCH IN MOTION	RIMM	B-	66.74	514.45 / 98	96.22 / 98	502.54
ACS-TECH80 LTD	ACSEF	B-	9.39	503.06 / 98	44.77 / 91	491.15
OMTOOL LTD	OMTL	D-	9.65	475.64 / 98	29.13 / 82	463.73
TRM CORP	TRMM	C	15.81	435.65 / 98	100.04 / 98	423.74
ALDILA INC	ALDA	C	10.69	426.89 / 98	27.39 / 80	414.98
FIRST HORIZON PHARMACEUTICAL	FHRX	C	17.00	421.52 / 98	-9.63 / 29	409.61
SHILOH INDUSTRIES INC	SHLO	C+	16.04	419.11 / 98	32.80 / 85	407.20
EVCI CAREER COLLEGES INC	EVCI	C+	10.21	409.85 / 98	122.47 / 99	397.94
SMTEK INTERNATIONAL INC	SMTI	C-	7.30	396.43 / 97	-6.12 / 32	384.52
EFJ INC	EFJI	B	8.33	380.57 / 97	188.56 / 99	368.66
MANNING GREG AUCTIONS INC	GMAI	B	14.00	371.22 / 97	87.10 / 97	359.31
CAL-MAINE FOODS INC	CALM	B	14.09	365.47 / 97	93.69 / 98	353.56
BLUE COAT SYSTEMS INC	BCSI	D+	26.52	365.35 / 97	20.00 / 72	353.44
CARRIER ACCESS CORP	CACS	C	13.10	365.05 / 97	48.19 / 92	353.14
NOVATEL WIRELESS INC	NVTL	C	23.83	364.15 / 97	46.29 / 91	352.24
INTELLIGROUP INC	ITIG	C-	5.15	360.91 / 97	72.95 / 96	349.00
TRAVELZOO INC	TZOO	C	27.09	352.50 / 97	———	340.59
OLYMPIC STEEL INC	ZEUS	B	17.45	343.46 / 97	68.69 / 95	331.55
INTERNATIONAL ASSETS HLDG CP	IAAC	C	9.81	341.36 / 97	66.47 / 95	329.45
UROLOGIX INC	ULGX	C	13.44	330.82 / 97	0.14 / 39	318.91
MGP INGREDIENTS INC	MGPI	B	35.56	329.66 / 97	56.07 / 94	317.75
HANSEN NATURAL CORP	HANS	A	20.60	329.54 / 97	78.69 / 97	317.63

Data date 07/16/04. For the most recent version of this list, please visit www.WeissRatings.com, go to "Products" and click on "Stocks."

Kathleen thinks about everything she has learned. Rounding another bend in the road, she and our Wise Guide spot a few wild animals in the distance. Now's a good time to talk in more detail about risk as the two of them look at those fearsome creatures from a (safe!) distance.

Chapter 15

Laugh at the (Risk) Traps — Use These Wise Tips

Risk involves more than your own personal comfort zone. There are four types of external risk that can affect your investment — so be aware! Pay particular attention to the four wise ways you can face them.

1. Business and Industry Risk

The company has an unexpected fall-off in business, related to either its operations or the industry as a whole.

2. Inflation Risk

Your investment earns 10% a year. Great! Suppose this year inflation is 4%, which means you now have really only earned 6%. If the economy struggles next year, and your investment earns only 6%, and inflation climbs to 6% too, that means you earn nada. If, however, your stock surges 20%, and inflation is only 4%, you are 16% ahead.

3. Liquidity Risk

There are two kinds of liquidity risk: one occurs when you can't sell an

Survival Tip
Diversification

In real estate, it's location, location, location. With stocks, it's diversify, diversify, diversify. This D-word is the mantra. Select stocks from different companies and industries, because industries have different cycles and events that cause price declines at different times. If you own stocks in various industries, a decline in one company would be offset by the improvement in another company.

Survival Tip
Inflation Risk

All investments are affected by inflation risk. The good news is that stocks do the best among other types of investments in keeping up with inflation.

investment because you can't find a buyer — something that rarely happens with the types of stocks you will invest in as a beginner. The second occurs when you, the investor, are short on cash for everyday living and are forced to sell your stocks when you otherwise would not have — perhaps at a time when the price is down but you expect it to rebound.

4. Market Risk

The fourth type of risk occurs when the market goes through a tough time. That's when you'll hear it called the "bear" market or a prolonged period of declining stock prices. That's what it did recently, catching a lot of investors off guard. We're talking about the bear market that scared Wall Street from March 2000 to October 2002. But even if there's a big, bad bear prowling around, there are ways you can protect yourself, stay invested, and ultimately prosper.

No matter how badly the market acts, you can correct its behavior — and protect your stock investment — with one of our Survival Tips. For more information from Weiss Ratings founder,

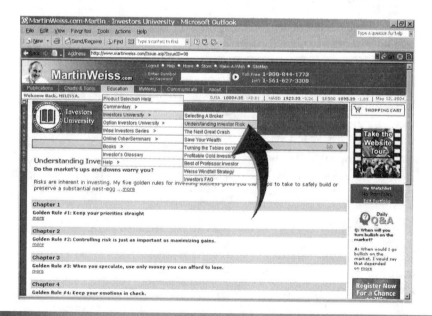

Martin Weiss, turn to Appendix B and read about risk in his amazing "Four Golden Rules." You can also log on to **www.MartinWeiss.com** and attend class virtually ("Understanding Investor Risk,") by accessing the "Education" bar from the top menu and dragging your mouse over "Investors University."

Chapter 16

You'll Need a Trader's Help

When you're ready to purchase shares of stock, you've got to continue a little further on your journey, making your way to the outpost deep in the jungle. Here you'll find a supply trader waiting to sell you the provisions you'll need for the rest of your safari. Think of the stock exchanges that way: a bunch of these outpost supply traders shouting and yelling for your broker's attention. Only in the real world of stock investing, of course, they're standing at the stock exchange, not in the jungle.

(Although we think the jungle metaphor works pretty well here!)

You may have heard of the New York Stock Exchange (NYSE) in lower Manhattan, which is the most widely known exchange. It's the stock "supermarket" where the nation's largest companies have historically sold their shares and it's the largest of the stock exchanges.

There's also the American Stock Exchange, or AMEX, which is composed of exchanges in Boston, Chicago, Cincinnati, Philadelphia, and San Francisco. These are called "listed" exchanges, because brokers list the shares of stock they have to buy or want to sell. Stock is bought and sold on the floors of these exchanges, with the exception of the NASDAQ (National Association of Securities Dealers Automatic Quotation System), which is, as its name spells out, an automated system. Recently, the AMEX merged with the NASDAQ.

Do you need a broker? YES!

A stock exchange is like a supermarket, but instead of buying groceries, you buy stock. To continue the analogy: The supermarket you go to depends on the stock you're buying. And, just like a supermarket, you get to pick what you want from any of the shelves, but you've got to check out at the register. The attendant at the checkout counter (called a broker in the world of stock investing) rings up your purchase, which also includes some money to pay his or her commission.

It would be very impractical if every investor who wanted to buy or sell stock had to travel to the exchanges to trade stock. Besides, you can't. You have to be licensed to buy or sell stock on the exchange. That's where brokers come in.

By definition, brokers are people who bring buyers and sellers together. There are all kinds of brokers: insurance brokers, mortgage brokers, real estate brokers, concert ticket brokers, and many more. We're just talking about stock brokers. Brokers must register with the NASD (National Association of Securities Dealers) in order to do business. A broker acts on your behalf, as the buyer, to find another broker who's working on someone else's behalf, as the seller. It's this broker's job to bring the two together.

Deserves Another Look
Investing Readiness

For a quiz focusing strictly on your risk tolerance for online trading, check out "Quiz: Are You Ready?" on the website of the Investing Online Resource Center (www.investingonline.org), funded by the North American Securities Administrators Association (NASAA), a nonprofit organization of state administrators who track the activity of brokers in their states.

So if you're looking to buy stock, you would place your order through a broker at either a full-service, discount, or online brokerage firm.

How does the broker on the floor of an exchange know what you want to buy or sell?

Good question! He or she gets an order on the computer screen from your broker in the office. This order tells the broker on the floor which stock you'd like him to buy or sell on your behalf. You can also park yourself at your computer and place your order online with a broker.

Selecting the right broker is as important as selecting the right stock investment. There are two key questions you have to answer for yourself before you choose a broker:

How much customer service do I want?

How much am I willing to pay in fees?

Keep these questions in mind as you read about the three types of brokers available:

1. Full-service Broker Offering Investment Advice or Portfolio Management

This broker offers a full range of trading services and financial advice and charges you a commission. As the name says, it's full service — for a price. The broker makes money based, not on how well your portfolio does, but by how often you trade. Most, but not all, of the brokers in this category provide specific recommendations on buying or selling stock. However, some brokers, especially those affiliated with banks, may also offer financial consulting regarding your portfolio and sector allocation.

2. Discount Broker Offering Low Commission Rates and Limited Services

This broker will execute your trades at a discounted commission rate, but offers no guidance in selecting stock. Some full-service brokers may also be listed as discount brokers because they offer a commission discount on any trades that you initiate.

Be On The Lookout
Commissions

Shop around for the best commissions. Commission costs can have a dramatic impact on your portfolio's performance.

3. Online Broker Offering Internet-based Trades and Research

This broker offers discounted trading via its website. Online brokers typically cater to the "do-it-yourself" crowd by offering research tools, but no advice or even contact with an actual broker.

Yikes! How do you decide whether to deal with a broker from a full-service or discount brokerage firm? Arm yourself with as much information as possible.

Consider the advantages and disadvantages:

Advantages of Full-Service Firms:

▲ **"One-stop Shopping"** – You can more readily trade other instruments, in addition to stocks, as you become more experienced and potentially want to venture into more sophisticated investments.

▲ **More Service** – Typically, but not always, a full-service broker will know more about your personal situation and be able to help you with your investment choices.

Disadvantages of Full-Service Firms:

▲ **Higher Commissions** – The standard commissions charged by full-service brokerage firms can be significantly higher than those charged by discount firms.

▲ **Stricter Requirements** – Many full-service firms are stricter, requiring a high net worth for riskier investments in things like options and futures. For most beginning investors this is not an issue.

Advantages of Discount and Online Brokerage Firms:

▲ **Discount Commissions** – Standard commissions are lower across the board. You may sometimes be able to negotiate still lower commission rates.

▲ **More Flexible Requirements** – The net worth requirements for opening an account are usually less strict than they are at full-service brokerage firms. Again, this is typically for riskier investing and not generally an issue for the beginning investor who's only buying and selling common stocks.

Disadvantage of Discount and Online Brokerage Firms:

▲ **Less Service** – Some investors see discount brokers as "order takers" who don't give you the time and service you need. This is true up to a point, but it's changing. To keep up with competition, many discount brokers are becoming more service oriented.

Be On The Lookout
Broker Guarantees

Your new broker tells you that the market is going to jump 25% this year. But, no one can guarantee returns. Do your homework. (And stop doing business with this broker!)

Yes, there's a lot to think about. You wouldn't walk into a jungle without a Guide. Stock investing takes a certain amount of smart planning too. But it's really just a step-by-step process, from signing up with the right Guide to reading the map correctly and following the signs.

Chapter 17

Don't Get Stranded in the Jungle — Check Your Broker's Record!

A beginning investor logically thinks that finding a good stock is top priority. But finding the right broker is critical, too. Don't get caught short — check your broker's record before you start doing business.

How do you do that? We offer a few wise tips:

Investigate the Broker's and the Firm's Integrity.

Go to **www.nasdr.com** and click on "NASD BrokerCheck." From there click on "Look up a Broker/Dealer Firm or Individual." Read through and agree to the Terms and Conditions and then select "General Public/Individual Investor" from the

drop down menu. You can then search on either an individual broker or a firm to receive a report listing any private or regulatory actions against them. If a "maybe" appears under "Disclosure Events" on the left hand side then click on "Deliver Report" on the top of the screen to request a copy by email.

Be On The Lookout SIPC Members

Is the firm a member of the Securities Investor Protection Corporation (SIPC)? Almost all brokers are SIPC members. SIPC provides limited customer protection if a brokerage firm runs out of money. However, SIPC does not insure against losses if your stock declines in value. Also contact the Securities and Exchange Commission (www.sec.gov), which monitors the industry, to file a complaint.

While it isn't unusual for a broker to switch firms a few times in a career, frequent job hopping can be a sign of trouble.

If the broker has been involved in securities arbitrations, find links to state securities regulators by visiting **www.nasaa.org**, the site of the North American Securities Administrators Association. State regulators can send you Central Registration Depository (CRD) reports, which offer a more detailed disciplinary record than those NASD provides. Call the phone number listed at your state regulators' website to request a broker's CRD report. Unfortunately, states don't offer this information online. The report may take weeks to arrive, but it's usually worth waiting for. It often lists complaints that don't appear on the NASD website.

Shop Around For the Best Commissions.

Commission costs can have a dramatic impact on an investment's performance. Most investors often ignore or underestimate how much of an impact broker commissions can have on their final results. Avoid disaster simply by using a broker who charges you the average commission rate.

To give you a head start in selecting one that suits your needs, we've put together the Broker Comparison Checklist on the next page. Although commissions alone shouldn't be the only factor that you consider when selecting a firm, these costs certainly can be a very critical factor if you trade actively.

Make sure the broker trades the same types of securities you want to trade. For example, you may want to trade preferred stock, which not all brokerage firms trade.

Be On The Lookout
Broker Check-Up

After selecting a broker, **keep close tabs on what he or she is doing.** Follow up within a day or two after making a trade to make sure your broker carried out your instructions properly. Also, check your monthly account statements carefully to make sure the transactions accurately reflect your orders. If there's an error, follow up immediately, first with your broker and then with the branch manager. If you get no satisfaction, go to the firm's compliance department. If the problem is still unresolved, file a formal complaint with the firm, the SEC, the NASD, and the stock exchanges to which the firm belongs.

Broker Comparison Checklist

	Broker #1	Broker #2	Broker #3
Name			
Types of Services Offered:			
Full-Service Brokerage	❑	❑	❑
Discount Brokerage	❑	❑	❑
Online Brokerage	❑	❑	❑
Money Mgmnt/Fee-Based Accts	❑	❑	❑
Mutual Fund Trading	❑	❑	❑
Annuities	❑	❑	❑
IRA Retirement Planning	❑	❑	❑
Other	❑	❑	❑
Commission/Fee Information:			
100 shares @ $10 per share	$_____	$_____	$_____
Full-Service Trade	$_____	$_____	$_____
Discount Trade	$_____	$_____	$_____
Online Trade	$_____	$_____	$_____
100 shares @ $100 per share			
Full-Service Trade	$_____	$_____	$_____
Discount Trade	$_____	$_____	$_____
Online Trade	$_____	$_____	$_____
1,000 shares @ $20 per share			
Full-Service Trade	$_____	$_____	$_____
Discount Trade	$_____	$_____	$_____
Online Trade	$_____	$_____	$_____
Additional Fees:			
Inactivity Fee	$_____	$_____	$_____
Account Minimum Fee	$_____	$_____	$_____
Other fees	$_____	$_____	$_____
Initial Minimum Investment	$_____	$_____	$_____
Licensed to Operate in My State	Yes__No__	Yes__No__	Yes__No__

Interview Your Broker.

Read the "10 Questions to Ask Your Broker" provided in this chapter. These questions are business-like and to the point. If you feel uncomfortable, print them out and send them to your broker in advance of meeting face to face.

Also, make sure your personality matches the broker's personality. Are you comfortable with the broker's style? Is he or she easy to reach? Is he or she knowledgeable and able to explain concepts clearly? Does the firm have a responsive customer service department so you can easily get answers to important questions and concerns?

Most important of all — REMEMBER THAT THE BROKER WORKS FOR YOU. You are paying him through your trading commission. Therefore, he must satisfy your needs and requests. Do not be intimidated by your broker. If you feel uncomfortable or intimidated, change to another broker right away.

You've traveled the ups and downs of the trail, and done a good job. We're going to sit down in the shade for a spell. After a quick break, you're ready to buy your first stock.

10 Questions to Ask Your Broker

Although your broker is supposed to be working on your behalf, there is an inherent flaw in the brokerage system: The bulk of a broker's compensation comes from the commissions he generates. So the more he gets you to buy, the more money he makes. While most brokers simply try to make a decent, honest living, the system inevitably rewards those who are aggressively looking out for the interests of the firm while penalizing those who prioritize the interests of the customer.

Your best defense is to arm yourself with as much information as you can when choosing and dealing with a broker. To that end, here are 10 questions you should ask. Keep in mind though, that unless you ask these questions specifically, your broker will probably never tell you.

Question #1:
What investment training have you had?

You're likely to hear your broker hem and haw over this answer. The answer you want to hear is that your broker has *formal* training, such as a degree in finance or accounting, or at the minimum a comprehensive training program at his firm. Most brokers are primarily salespeople, and many have not had *any* financial training aside from how to sell the firm's products.

The brokerage firms do make an effort to weed out truly inept individuals. But again, the system works against them. They need bodies to generate commissions, and after investing time and money to train salespeople, they're likely to err on the side of keeping as many as possible, including the borderline and marginal.

Question #2:
Do you receive extra commissions
for selling house products?

For years, brokers were given free trips, expensive gifts and just extra money to sell "in-house" mutual funds to their clients. Dean Witter and Prudential are just two of the major brokerage houses that have gotten into trouble with the regulators for pushing their own in-house products over other investments.

And despite regulators best efforts to crack down on this practice, it still continues. So, be sure to ask your broker to give you the performance history of the product he's pushing. Then go to your local library and review Weiss Ratings' *Guide to Stock Mutual Funds* for an evaluation of the fund's risk-adjusted performance.

Question #3:
Is your firm underwriting this stock?

Most firms, even the smaller regional ones, have some investment banking business. In other words, they help companies sell their stock to the public for a fee, such as through an initial public offering (IPO). There's nothing wrong with this since it's simply the manner in which companies raise capital.

The problem arises when brokers are asked to support the investment banking side of the business by promoting those same stocks to their customers, an obvious conflict of interest. The stocks are rarely worth the buzz, and often get dumped on the public with disastrous results. So, you need to find out if the firm is underwriting any of the stock offerings for the company it's recommending.

Question #4:
Do your research analysts cover some of the same companies that the firm underwrites?

Brokerage firms are supposed to maintain a "Chinese Wall," which clearly separates their research departments from their underwriting departments. It is illegal for these departments to know what the other is doing, before the information becomes public. However, in reality, the Chinese Wall is easily penetrated. It is not uncommon for research analysts to be forced to write a glowing report on a company that their brokerage firm is taking public ... or to suppress a negative research report which the firm fears could hurt its underwriting business.

Furthermore, those same research analysts are under pressure to promote these companies to their retail brokers, who, in turn, are under pressure to sell them to their brokerage clients. Investment banking firms are required to perform what is called "due diligence" — a serious and comprehensive review of a company — before they decide to underwrite its stock. But they are also under tremendous pressure to bring in big underwriting fees. Consequently, sometimes their due diligence is not so diligent.

Question #5:
Do you have a quota to meet for selling the stock in the companies that your firm underwrites?

Brokerage firms typically assist their underwriting clients with "dog and pony shows." This is where the investment bankers — and often the research analysts as well — hold special meetings for the firm's brokers or visit the branch offices of the brokerage firm to hawk the new stock. There is tremendous pressure on the brokers to sell these stocks to their clients. Many are even required to sell a certain quota of shares. Ask your broker about this. You won't get an honest answer every time, but it can't hurt to try.

Question #6:
Does your firm have its own trading account?

Most firms trade stocks for themselves as well as for their clients. You can tell if a brokerage firm has a trading account by looking at its income statement, so don't be bashful about asking for a copy of the statement. You won't be able to tell which stocks are in the firm's trading account, though, which leads to the next question.

Question #7:
Do you currently hold this stock in your firm's principal trading account?

If your broker is honest, he'll tell you the truth. And if you find out the firm does hold the stock in its trading account, you should probably decline the broker's advice, or at a minimum, get a second opinion from another source. Chances are the firm is just trying to clean out its own portfolio of stocks that haven't done well for them.

Question #8:
Are you selling this stock on behalf of one of your major clients? If so, why is he selling and how many shares is he selling?

Sometimes, a major customer of a brokerage firm wants to unload a sizable holding of a losing stock. And because he is a very good customer of the firm — generating a lot of commissions — the firm is going to try to accommodate him. But they have to find buyers for that stock, so they try to push it on their smaller customers who may not know that the stock is a loser. It helps to know how much of this stock is on the block, who is selling it, and *why*.

Question #9 (when buying through a bank or Savings & Loan): Is this investment insured by the FDIC?

Stocks, bonds, and mutual funds are *not* federally insured for market losses. The Securities Investors Protection Corporation (SIPC) insures investments only if a company goes out of business, and even then, you only get the current market value. But when stock or mutual funds are sold through a bank, investors are sometimes led to believe that these investments *do* fall under the FDIC guarantee. Dean Witter and NationsBank were heavily fined for not telling their customers that the funds they bought at their friendly neighborhood bank were not part of the FDIC's insurance program.

Many bank customers think that whatever they buy at the bank is covered by the same FDIC insurance coverage. And unfortunately many mutual funds don't make an adequate effort to dissuade customers of this notion.

Question #10:
What about Dividend Reinvestment Plans (DRIPS)? Wouldn't I save a lot of money buying stocks this way?

The correct answer is "Yes." Unfortunately, many brokers will never tell you about it. Some may even try to discourage you by saying you have to wait too long to actually buy the shares, or that you can't get them at the price you want. Reason: There are no commissions in it for them.

The truth is that DRIPS can be very profitable investments for many people. About 1,100 companies traded on US stock exchanges have DRIPS. After you buy the initial share, you can then buy additional shares right through the company or its agent. This can save you a ton of money in commissions. Sometimes you are charged a small fee; other times the plan allows you to buy shares at no fee whatsoever. In either event, the savings are significant. You can even set up many of these plans for automatic transfer from your bank account. Your dividends are automatically reinvested.

There is a downside, though. You can't specify at what price you want to buy the shares because your money is pooled with that of other investors, and the company buys shares on a regular schedule. But if you're investing for the long-term, you shouldn't be overly concerned about market timing.

For more information on DRIPS, refer to the *Directory of Companies Offering Dividend Reinvestment Plans*, 14th Edition by Sumie Kinoshita, Evergreen Enterprises. Order by calling (301) 549-3939 for $36.95 plus shipping. You can also check *The Guide to Direct Investment Plans*, the Moneypaper, by calling (800) 388-9993 or at **www.directinvesting.com** for $27.00. Check out the Moneypaper at **www.moneypaper.com**.

Also, on the Internet, you can go to **www.enrolldirect.com** to access "The Clearinghouse for Direct Purchase Plans" ... or call them at (800) 774-4117. You can use this free service to request enrollment materials from companies and manufacturers that offer direct purchase programs.

Chapter 18

Put in Your Market Order

W hen you're ready to buy your first stock, it helps to know that there are several different types of orders you can place, and they each work differently. The goal here is to make your money work for you, and protect your profits. So which type do you choose?

Market Order

This is the most basic type: A market order tells your broker to buy or sell a stock at the current market price. It tends to be immediately filled, because it has no limitations or restrictions. A market order to buy is executed at what is known as the "ask" price, and a market order to sell is executed at what is known as the "bid" price. Market orders are guaranteed to fill, but they do not guarantee the price. A rapidly rising, or falling, market can lead to a "fill" price (the price at which the stock was sold or purchased) substantially different than what you expected when you entered the market order.

Limit Order

If you want to make sure to control any losses, you put in a limit order. As the name implies, a limit order sets a restriction on the purchase or selling price: a "buy" limit order sets the maximum amount you are willing to pay for the named stock; a "sell" limit order sets the minimum price you will take to sell a stock.

For example, suppose a broker recommends that you place a buy limit order at $5 on Company A's stock. This means that you'll only buy the stock if you can purchase it for $5 or less. If the price is (and stays) above $5, the order will not get filled. When you go to buy a car or a home, eventually you arrive at a price that you think is fair and of which you will not pay more. That's essentially a limit order. You might offer to pay $25,000 for a car, but no more. The dealership then can either fill your offer at (or below) the price, or not fill the order at all.

Using limit orders is a great way to buy a stock at a fair price. On the other end of the process, sell limits are a great way to try to lock in a higher profit rather than simply exiting at whatever price the market offers. The one downside to a limit order is that your order might not be executed if the target price is never reached.

Day Order

Another way to buy or sell stock is using the day order, which is an order that's good only for today. Using a day order will sometimes gain some extra leverage, because the brokerage house knows they only have today to get this order filled. A day limit order demands a fair price today, or the brokerage house risks losing this order. If you don't get your day order filled, you have to place a new day limit order the next day and again the following day until your order is executed. If you place this order after market hours, it's good through the close of trading the next day.

Good Till Canceled

With this type of order, your order remains in effect until either it is executed or you cancel it. The order will automatically execute when the stock price reaches its target stated in your limit order. For example, if you have a "good till canceled" order to sell XYZ when it hits $120 a share, the order will execute automatically when the price reaches that point. Once a "good till canceled" order is placed, you must expressly cancel it if you wish to change something about the order. Not all brokerage firms will support "good till canceled" orders, and each has its own limits on how long it will maintain such an order. Check with your broker for details.

Stop-Loss Order

This type of order is a sell order, which means you tell your broker to sell your stock if the price drops below a specified price. Most of the time, you put in this type of order to protect the profits already earned on a stock.

Survival Tip
Length of Investment

Stay invested longer. Economic cycles last at least five years. Staying invested over several economic cycles increases your chances of long-term growth. Also, diversifying across other asset classes, like cash and bonds, helps to reduce your risk to the stock market.

You've shopped, but hopefully, you haven't dropped! It's important to learn to pace yourself, especially with stock investing. You want to go the distance, and you're ready for the next exciting step …

Chapter 19

Set Up Your Camp

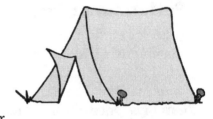

Portfolio is simply a fancy name for the collection of investments you own. It could contain one stock, or 20 stocks, or any combination of stocks, bonds, and cash. Of course, here we are focusing on the portion of your portfolio that you've chosen to invest in stocks — your stock portfolio.

Ideally, you want to have roughly an even amount of money invested in each of the stocks you own. The only exception to this is if you're just starting to invest and only buying small amounts at a time. In that case, you would want to continue to invest those small amounts until you get to, say, 50 or 100 shares of a particular stock and then start saving for the next stock. But if you have enough money right away to invest in several stocks, remember that you should diversify by purchasing stocks from different industries or sectors.

A general rule of thumb is that you are adequately diversified if you own 10 or 15 stocks of different types, in different sectors (healthcare, consumer goods, energy, etc.) and of different sizes (small-, medium-, and large "cap" companies, meaning companies of different sizes).

If you consider yourself conservative, you should make up your portfolio of stocks with a Weiss Risk Rating of B or higher. If you have a moderate tolerance for risk, you should make up your portfolio of stocks with a Weiss Risk Rating of C+, C, or C-. If you are aggressive, you should make up your portfolio of stocks with a Weiss Risk Rating of D+, D, or D-. If you would like to obtain an updated list of samples of stocks that fall into these risk categories, please visit www.WeissRatings.com, go to "Products" and click on "Stocks." To purchase a Weiss Investment Rating, please visit **www.WeissRatings.com** or call **1-800-289-9222**.

Our Overall Ratings are broken down into two major components:

Performance Rating

A stock's Performance Rating is based on its total return to shareholders over the last four years and its prospects for future returns based on sales, net income, earnings trends, and economic factors. In addition, we look at valuations (i.e., price to earnings, price to sales, and price to book), based on the stock's current price. Returns and trends are weighted to give more recent performance greater emphasis. Thus, two stocks may have given back the same returns to their shareholders over the past four years, but the one with the better performance in the last 12 months gets a slightly higher performance rating.

Risk Rating

We base this rating on the level of volatility in the stock's daily and monthly returns and on the underlying company's financial stability, as well as economic factors. Stocks with more volatility relative to other common stocks are considered riskier, and thus receive a lower risk rating. By contrast, stocks with very stable returns are considered less risky and receive a higher risk rating. Likewise, companies with weak financial stability are riskier investments than those that are financially sound. We also consider stocks that appear to be overvalued at their current prices. Please note that we don't give any of the stocks that we rate a risk rating of A. Why? Because all stock investments, by their very nature, involve at least some degree of risk.

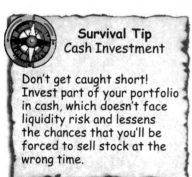

**Survival Tip
Cash Investment**

Don't get caught short! Invest part of your portfolio in cash, which doesn't face liquidity risk and lessens the chances that you'll be forced to sell stock at the wrong time.

… and then ultimately, the …

Overall Investment Rating

The Overall Investment Rating we give a stock is based on a combination of the Performance Rating and Risk Rating. Together these factors reflect our opinion about a stock's historical risk-adjusted performance and its value relative to the company's earnings prospects.

Keeping Your Eye on the Prize

As soon as you start purchasing stocks, you should track their performance. You can do this easily and register free of charge on **www.MartinWeiss.com**. Here's how:

▲ Click on "Charts & Tools" and go down to "Portfolio Manager." Then click on 'Add a Portfolio.' This will take you to a worksheet where you will enter the information for the stocks you want to track.

The first block will appear as 'Symbol.'

▲ Enter the ticker symbol of the stock you want to follow.

▲ Next, enter the number of shares you purchased.

▲ Then enter the price you paid for each share.

▲ And the total commission you paid to the brokerage firm for the purchase of that specific stock

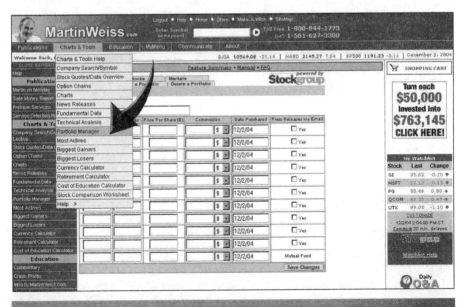

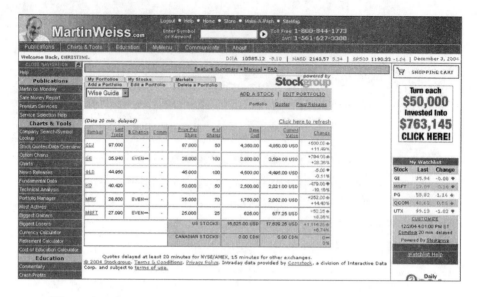

▲ Then finally the date you purchased the shares.

▲ If you wish to receive press releases on your stock via e-mail, check yes. Otherwise just leave the box blank.

▲ Now click on "Save Changes." Your settings will be saved so you can check back whenever you like and not have to re-enter everything.

After you've clicked on "Save Changes," it will take you to a page that tells you the current value of your stock and how much money you have gained or lost. From there, you can also look at "Press Releases" to keep up with each of your stocks and also add more stocks or make any change to what you've already entered. You can also check the stock listings of your local paper for basic information. The following page displays a sample of what you may find in your newspaper.

So tell us the truth — that wasn't as bad as you thought, was it?

In fact, right about now, you're wondering, what was the big deal, after all, with stock investing?

The answer, which might surprise you:

It's not that hard to get started — the challenge is staying in the game!

NYSE, Amex, Nasdaq
Stock Exchanges

N = NYSE Q=NASDAQ A=AMEX

Exc.: Exchange the stock is traded in

Chg.: The $ change in the price at the closing of the most recent trading day from the close of the previous trading day

Name: Ticker symbol of the stock

Last: The closing price of the stock on the most recent trading day

A

Name	Exc.	Last	Chg.
AAG 2033 n	N	24.75	-0.09
▼AAG 2034 n	N	24.40	-0.05
AAON	Q	20.23	+0.08
			+0.49
			+0.20
ABM	N	18.58	+0.12
ABN Amro	N	22.21	+0.27
ABN pfE	N	23.25	+0.33
ABN pfF	N	24.40	+0.41
ABN pfG	N	23.79	+0.04
ACMoore	Q	28.49	+0.49
ACE Cap	N	25.99	+0.02
ACE Ltd	N	43.21	+0.56
ACE pfC	N	27.00	+0.11
ACM Op	N	8.11	-0.02
ACM Inco	N	7.82	-0.11
ACMMD	N	7.67	-0.09
ACMMu	N	11.75	...
ACS Tc80	Q	10.65	-0.81
ADECp	Q	20.43	-0.11
AEP Ind	Q	11.94	+0.14
AES Cp	N	7.70	-0.06
AES pfC	N	41.30	-0.15
AEW RE	A	15.76	+0.01
AFLAC	N	41.15	-0.15
AGCO	N	21.12	+0.27
AGLCap pf	N	26.29	+0.03
AGL Res	N	28.71	+0.25
AK Steel	N	5.31	-0.15
AMB Fnl s	Q	18.00	+0.50
AMB Pr	N	31.47	+0.31
AMB pfL	N	24.50	-0.30
AMB pfM	N	23.80	+0.25
AMC	A	16.54	+0.14
AMIS Hld n	Q	16.07	-0.16
AMLI Rs	N	26.43	+0.33
AMN Hlth	N	17.68	-0.35
AMR	N	12.36	-0.14
AMR Cp 39	N	20.00	+0.30
AMX Cp	Q	10.79	+0.08
ASA Ltd	N	36.98	-0.30
ASBC pfA	N	26.09	-0.02
ASE Tst	Q	9.49	-0.94
ASM Intl	Q	21.60	-0.29
ASML Hld	Q	16.69	+0.06
ASV Inc	Q	33.52	-0.01
AT&T	N	18.14	-0.17

Name	Exc.	Last	Chg.
Albemar	N	30.?3	+0.43
Alberto s	N	47.?	+0.37
Albertsn	N	23.6?	+0.?
Alcan	N	42.7?	
Alcatel	N	15.8?	
Alcide	Q	20.53	
Alcoa	N	32.30	
Alcon	N	75.30	
▲Alderwds	Q	12.42	
Aldila rs	Q	5.79	
AlexBld	Q	33.52	+0.60
Alexdr	N	157.70	+2.45
AlexREE	N	58.15	+0.77
Allco	Q	34.50	+0.83
AlignTech	Q	18.95	-0.03
Alkerm	Q	16.18	+0.18
AlliASem	Q	9.33	-0.07
AllegCp	N	264.95	-0.25
AllgEngy	N	14.43	-0.04
AllegTch	N	11.55	...
▲Allergan	N	91.77	+0.33
Allete	N	35.84	+0.07
AlliAMkt	N	15.98	+0.23
AlliAtl g	Q	18.77	+0.11
AlliancB s	Q	15.50	-0.15
AlliCAMun	N	13.30	-0.02
AlliCap	N	35.42	+0.22
AlliData	N	36.50	+0.05
AllncFnc	Q	28.27	-0.23
AlliGam	N	26.70	-0.36
AlliNtlMun	N	13.45	+0.03
▼AlliNYMun	N	12.90	+0.04
▲AllnceRes	Q	40.70	+1.48
AllianSemi	Q	6.47	-0.14
AllWrld	N	11.30	+0.02
AllWrld2	N	11.38	...
AlliantEgy	N	25.60	...
▲AlliantTch	N	62.17	+0.07
Allianz	N	10.96	+0.08
AlliedCap	N	24.76	-0.64
AlldDefnse	A	20.00	+0.01
AldDmcq	N	33.16	-0.20
AlldHlthcr	Q	5.98	-0.02
AldHlPd	Q	6.09	+0.04
AlldHldg	A	6.05	+0.03
Aldirish	N	29.85	-0.20
AlliedMot	Q	5.17	-0.32
AldWaste	N	13.05	+0.02
AldWst pfC	N	71.90	...
AllmrFn	N	35.95	+1.02
AllmrST	N	9.12	...
AllosThera	**Q**	**5.06**	**+0.77**
Allscripts	Q	9.20	-0.85
Allstate	N	46.82	+0.41
AllstrmB g	Q	56.00	-0.23
Alltel	N	51.7?	...

Name	Exc.	Last	Chg.
Anaren	Q	17.44	-0.81
AncBWI	Q	24.65	-0.24
Anheusr	N	51.98	+0.03
AnikaTh	Q	9.72	+0.12
Anixter	N	29.71	+0.48
ansmink	Q	7.25	+0.15
Ansys	Q	39.36	-0.44
Anteon	N	33.45	+0.55
Anthem	N	93.34	+0.49
Anthem un	N	108.08	+0.16
AnthCap	N	10.98	+0.01
AnthCa pfC	N	25.55	-0.04
Antigncs	Q	10.29	+0.18
Anworth	N	12.70	-0.02
Aon Corp	N	26.61	+0.12
Apache s	N	44.27	+1.33
Aptinv	N	28.41	+0.22
Aptinv pfD	N	24.95	-0.17
Aptinv pfG	N	26.00	-0.08
Aptinv pfQ	N	26.09	-0.04
Aptinv pfR	N	26.00	...
Aptinv pfT	N	24.60	...
Aptinv pfU	N	23.75	+0.05
Apex	N	8.08	-0.01
ApexSilv	A	17.43	-0.48
Aphton	Q	5.69	+0.47
ApogeeE	Q	11.92	+0.22
Apogee s	A	8.65	...
ApogentT	N	32.42	-0.39
ApolloG	Q	93.25	-1.85
▼Apollolnv n	Q	13.58	-0.42
AppleC	Q	26.94	-0.19
Applebees	Q	38.31	+0.17
Applica	N	12.43	-0.08
ApplBio	N	18.69	-0.14
AppFlms	Q	26.39	+0.06
Apldlndl	N	26.13	-0.75
ApldMatl	Q	19.27	-0.17
AMCC	Q	5.27	-0.18
ApldSig	Q	26.68	+0.19
Applix	Q	5.26	+0.11
Apria	N	29.40	+0.07
Aptargp	N	40.00	-0.95
AquaAm s	N	20.97	+0.04
aQuantive	Q	10.04	...
Aquila32	N	22.24	+0.04
ArQule	Q	7.57	-0.22
Aracm	N		

Buying a stock isn't the end of the trail — it's a whole new adventure. Smart investors monitor their stocks and make sure that they continue to be good investments. For more information, turn to pages 127-129 in Chapter 20.

There are only three wise tips you need to follow.

Stay Ahead of the Market with These Three Steps

T here are three steps, and only three, you
need to review after you've set
up your portfolio. They're really not
hard at all:

Step #1: Keep on Track.

Once you set up your portfolio, monitor its
performance regularly.

You just bought a new home. Was the sale the
end of the process? Not at all! To keep up your
investment, you do regular maintenance. In fact,
regular maintenance helps you grow the investment you made in your home. It's the same with the stocks you
begin to invest in. It's called **rebalancing.** Reviewing your
portfolio from time to time is the most important thing you can
do. Once every quarter is enough. Don't go nuts. Is rebalancing
hard to do? Do you have a car? Every year or so, you need to
redistribute the wear and tear on the tires, because some can
take all the travel — and perform better — and some can't.

It's the same with stock investing: Say you have a total stock
portfolio of $15,000, of which you decided to invest $5,000 in
Coca-Cola Co., $5,000 in Dell, and $5,000 in Home Depot —
1/3 in each. Assume that Home Depot has a great year, and
now the Home Depot portion of your portfolio has grown to
$10,000, while the Coca-Cola Co. and Dell stock have each
grown to just $6,000. Now you have 45% of your total portfolio

in Home Depot alone with only 27% each in Coca-Cola Co. and Dell. Your portfolio no longer has the same proportion of each stock as it did at the start. To rebalance your total portfolio, you will have to sell some Home Depot and invest the proceeds in more Coca-Cola Co. and Dell or in a totally new stock. That means you have to redistribute a portion of the Home Depot profits to other stocks.

Why is rebalancing important? Because the stock market is a living, breathing, reality; it changes from day to day, and minute to minute. You don't have to stay on top of the changes in your portfolio every nanosecond (in fact, you would drive yourself crazy doing so), but a quarterly checkup is smart thinking. It's what the professionals do for their important clients, and now you can too. Rebalance for your most important client: you!

Step #2: Keep Score

Periodically check your stock portfolio to see how it's doing. Is it still in line with your investment goals and risk tolerance?

Checking quarterly is prudent. Check a stock's performance by logging on to **www.MartinWeiss.com**.

Step #3: Keep Informed

Ever see a Wall Street trader on a business trip, lugging a brief-case with what looks like 20 pounds of reading material? You don't need to read that much, but you do need to keep informed.

Be On The Lookout
Performance

Don't chase performance! For many companies, being included in the S&P 500 is a big achievement, but there's an unpleasant surprise for the unsuspecting investor: not all stocks in the S&P 500 are good investments. There are good apples in the barrel, but also some rotten ones. Before you buy, check the Weiss Investment Rating.

Look at one or two popular investing magazines, and the *Wall Street Journal*, the industry's bible of stock investing, which looks at more stocks than any other source of information. Reading the newspaper will help you understand a bit more about where the market is going. Also read about your own investments. Keep up with news and look at the company's annual report, both of which are usually found on the company's website.

Other sources are the websites of the exchanges directly. (www.nyse.com, www.amex.com, and www.nasdaq.com). If you're really feeling ambitious, there are many websites (cnn.com, cbsmarketwatch.com) that carry news, and they often offer e-mail updates you can sign up for any time a company that interests you makes news.

But again, don't go nuts! The latest daily update from Wall Street on the evening news may not help you that much at all if the market has zoomed up — or down — dramatically. Remember, you're investing for the long haul.

If you've read this far, we've got only one more thing to say — congratulations! You made it to the other side of the jungle and you did an excellent job following the map, facing risk, and figuring out the clues. We hope this information helped you on the trail.

To let us know how you're doing, and how we can help you further, write us at
Weiss Ratings, Inc., PO Box 689608, Jupiter, FL 33468-9608
or email us at **comments@weissratings.com**.

To purchase a Weiss Investment Rating, visit us at **www.WeissRatings.com**, or give us a call at **800-289-9222**.

Appendix

Appendix A

13 Wise Warnings
Before You Invest Your First Dollar

Here's our list of tried-and-true tips to read — before you invest your first dollar. Some are so obvious, it doesn't seem we should mention them. But many beginning investors make these common mistakes — and there's a reason why there are 13 of them! The operative word here is "Don't"!

1. **Don't borrow money to fund your stock account.** Don't take cash advances on credit cards, or borrow money from friends or relatives. You don't need the added stress of collection calls or angry acquaintances if your investments don't go well. If you must borrow money, you probably shouldn't be trading stocks. Build up savings (and thus cash) as a foundation, before taking greater risk with stocks.

2. **Don't "bet it all" on any one trade, no matter how favorable it looks.** A few winners in a row, or a tip from an "indisputable source" makes some people put all of their account at risk by plunking it down on a single trade. Risk it all on one stock — and you can risk everything. Don't do it!

3. **Don't pay too much in broker commissions.** Shop around and find a good broker with competitive rates. If your commission costs are too high, you will need to make more money on the trade just to cover costs. Keep your transaction costs to a minimum by shopping around (see the worksheet on page 109). The lower your transaction cost, the closer you are to the territory all investors aim for: "net profit."

4. **Understand what "averaging down" is before you do it.** In a nutshell, averaging down means that you lower

the average price you've spent on a stock by purchasing more after your original investment declines in value. This means you were wrong about the direction of this stock (or you haven't been monitoring the stock closely enough during a slide) to begin with. If that's true, you might consider exiting the existing stock position too, take the losses, and move that money on to a more favorable position. There are strong arguments for taking either approach.

5. **Don't fall in love with one stock.** Even if you feel like you are an expert on a particular company, diversification is a key to investing success. It may be more prudent to spread your investment dollars around to several stocks (preferably in different sectors or industries). Remember the old saying: "Don't put all your eggs in one basket." It applies to smart stock investing too.

6. **Don't pay too much to enter a stock position.** Demand a fair price at entry and exit by using limit orders. You don't walk into a car dealership, select a car, and then tell the dealer that you are willing to pay any price for it, do you? The trading floor will be happy to collect any amount you are willing to pay above a fair price. But if you overpay, and the stock falls back to a fair value after other investors withdraw, you'll lose on your investment.

7. **Use other kinds of orders to control your broker.** In addition to limit orders, good until canceled, and day orders are handy tools, too.

8. **Don't let judgments in hindsight make you crazy.** The "perfect" entry and exit points are always easier to spot when looking at PAST prices and charts. Everyone is a perfect market timer when they have the benefit of hindsight. If you are able to perfectly time entry and exits in the present on all of your trades, you can do something that no other human has ever been able to do.

9. **Don't allow yourself to fall into the trap of moving targets.** You should NEVER be waiting "a little longer" to "see if the stock can go higher." Take profits at your preset profit target, or risk seeing a good profit be wiped away by volatile swings in trading. Greed is your enemy when you fall prey to this approach. Know your exit price before you enter each investment, and then exit at that price.

10. **Don't let fear or greed into your investing mindset.** Objectivity is a key to success. Keep emotions out of your decision-making.

11. **Don't let trading excitement override common sense.** Four winners in a row should not make you "double up" or bet it all on the fifth trade. Control this temptation of greed. When you enjoy the "rush" of a good number of wins in a row, you are probably outperforming the average stock investor. Keep Murphy's Law in mind when you are experiencing these "hot streaks."

12. **Don't overly resist taking losses.** Loss management is another key part of successful investing. Cut losses short and move on to other opportunities. While you can wait many years for a losing stock position to turn around or even become profitable, that is many years that the money in that position is held hostage. Could that money be better invested in some other position? All investors face losses in investing. It can be a very good strategy to take the loss and move on to a new opportunity.

13. **Don't rely on "luck" or "hope."** "I think this is my lucky day" is NOT a good foundation on which to risk money in new stock investments. Study the market, and the choices you're considering. If most of your rationale is based on luck or hope, you are probably not going to enjoy long-term success with stock investing.

Appendix B

Four Golden Rules on Reducing Investor Risk from Weiss Group Founder, Martin D. Weiss, Ph.D.

GOLDEN RULE #1
Keep your priorities straight:
Aim first for savings and capital preservation, second for growth, and third for speculative profits.

How do you put this rule into practice?

■ **Start immediately.** If you don't have a savings plan in place, the sooner you begin one, the better. Even at a low interest rate of just 2% per year:

> Saver A, who saves $1,000 per year beginning at age 25, will have $60,402 at age 65.

> Saver B, who saves $1,000 per year beginning at age 35, will have $40,568 at age 65.

As you can see, starting just 10 years earlier makes a huge difference. At age 65, Saver A has 49% more than Saver B. And when interest rates rise, the power of saving earlier will be magnified very significantly.

■ **Be consistent.** Figure out how much you can comfortably save each month. Many people aim too high, fail, and then give up. Better to aim low and then stick with it.

■ **Automate your savings.** If possible, set up a program to save automatically. Your employer, your credit union, or your bank can provide additional information.

- **Stick with safe institutions.** To preserve your savings or your nest egg, make sure it is kept at a safe bank, credit union, insurance company, brokerage firm, or money market fund. Wouldn't it be ironic — and heartbreaking — if, after all your diligence and care, your accumulated savings were threatened by a financial failure or mishap? To help you avoid that kind of disaster, check out the financial safety rating of your institutions at **www.WeissRatings.com**.

- **Use Treasuries.** Seriously consider short-term Treasury securities or Treasury-only money funds, despite the low yields they currently offer.

- **Don't confuse savings with investments.** Be sure to maintain a clear separation between the two. Investments inevitably expose your capital to some risk; savings are designed to protect your capital. Investments can be in stocks, stock mutual funds, or real estate that can go up or down. Savings should be limited to vehicles that are highly unlikely to go down in value. They prioritize the return of your money rather than the return on your money. With investments, it often makes sense to time the market; staying invested for at least five years. With savings, time is not as much of a factor. Consistency and regularity are more important than market timing.

GOLDEN RULE #2
Controlling risk is just as important as maximizing gains

We all have a natural tendency to focus on the spice and excitement of investing — the performance. There's nothing wrong with that — the profit potential can indeed be a very important driver of your ultimate success. However, the steps below to avoid and control risk are equally vital:

■ **Objectively evaluate your personal tolerance for risk.** Remember: An investment that may be suitable for someone else could be inappropriate for you, depending on how much risk you are comfortable taking, the number of years you have before retirement, your income level and tax rate, your other existing investments and personal net worth, plus your expectations about investment performance. So to help you evaluate each of these issues — and come up with a total "risk score," be sure to run through our investor quiz on pages 43-45 of this book. It will only take a few minutes, but it could make a great difference in your results and your peace of mind.

■ **Find out the risk level of each investment.** To find the Weiss Investment Rating on stocks that you are considering, look for *Weiss Ratings' Ultimate Guided Tour of Stock Investing* in the reference section of many public libraries. The quarterly guide lists ratings on more than 9,000 stocks, including all those traded on the New York Stock Exchange, the American Stock Exchange and Nasdaq. To purchase a rating, visit **www.WeissRatings.com** or call **1-800-289-9222**.

■ **Control your risk.** High-risk investments are not bad; often they are the outstanding performers. There's a place for risk — provided you take advantage of our tips that can help you control that risk. Specifically:

For investments that expose you to large potential losses, use stop-loss orders on investments that we feel may expose you to risk. If the value of your security falls, there is no guarantee that you will get a price that corresponds exactly to the stop-loss level we specify. But it should help protect your capital to a large extent — either to prevent a larger loss or to protect an open profit.

■ **Diversify beyond the stock market by investing in various asset classes.** Some people think that "diversification" means spreading your money among multiple stocks or stock market sectors. A truly diversified portfolio should also include money market funds, bonds, and cash.

- **Maintain a balanced portfolio.** Too many investment decisions are based on just one theory about the future direction of the market. Build a portfolio that should be able to handle multiple future outcomes.

GOLDEN RULE #3
When you speculate, use only money you can afford to lose

Far too many people speculate with the keep-safe portion of their nest egg. They fail to realize that speculation can ruin them just as easily as it can pay huge potential rewards. Some words of caution:

- Do not use funds that you'll need for emergencies, your children's or grandchildren's education, basic necessities, retirement living expenses, or long-term health care. One key danger signal to watch for: If you find yourself counting on the expected gains in order to make your financial plan a success, you have probably exceeded your limits.

- Even if you do have enough capital, do not speculate if you find yourself losing sleep over it.

- Similarly, do not speculate if it causes stress between you and your significant other, or threatens other family relationships. It's not worth it.

- Certainly do not speculate if you feel it's having a negative impact on your physical health.

- If you feel comfortable with various categories of aggressive investments, do take advantage of them. They have the potential to generate very handsome profits. Nevertheless, learn as much as you can about the risks inherent in each.

Small cap and penny stocks can often suffer from poor liquidity. If a small group of large investors — or a large number of small investors — rush to buy before you do, they can drive the price you pay far above its true value. As soon as that buying pressure subsides, the price can often fall back down sharply, leaving you with severe losses. Similarly, if there is a rush to sell, it can drive down the value of your shares despite no changes in the company's prospects. For more information on the risks of investing, visit the Securities Exchange Commission's (SEC) website (www.sec.gov).

Futures contracts offer very high leverage — the ability to effectively control large sums with a very small deposit. Therefore, relatively small moves in the market can bring about very large gains or losses. We do not provide futures trading recommendations. However, if you decide to play this game, be sure to learn all about the risks and the devices for controlling them, including stop losses and disciplined money management. For more information on the risks of futures, visit the website of the Commodity Futures Trading Commission (CFTC) (www.cftc.gov).

Options on securities: When you purchase "put" or "call" options on a stock or an index, and you stick strictly with options (never exercising them to hold positions in the underlying instruments), your risk is strictly limited to the amount you invest, plus the commission you pay your broker. However, your potential profits are not limited in any way. This can often provide a very favorable risk-reward ratio.

Indeed, provided you do not purchase expensive options, the risk limitation inherent in the option itself can often be enough to protect your capital, without the need for stop-loss orders.

However, if you continue to buy losing options, your losses can still pile up over a period of time. So, like with any other speculative investment, you must never invest more than you can afford to lose. For more information on the risk of options, visit the Chicago Board of Options Exchange (CBOE) website. (www.CBOE.com)

Options on futures: The same principles and rules apply as with options on securities. When you buy put or call options on a futures contract, your risk is strictly limited to the price you pay, plus commissions. There is just one exception: If you exercise the option, you will be holding an actual short or long position in the underlying futures contract, which, in turn, would expose you to risk that could be greater than your original investment. Therefore, to limit your exposure, you should stick with the options only, and instruct your broker accordingly.

GOLDEN RULE #4
Keep your emotions in check

No matter what aspect of your finances — your savings, your investments, your speculative portfolio — the ability to control emotions is a critical key to success.

If you let emotions get the better of you, your chances of success in any area can be greatly diminished. How do you stay unemotional, disciplined, and objective?

- **Treat your money as a business.** It's not a game. Consider your income as revenues. Categorize and keep track of your expenses, including broker' commissions and fees, as you would in any business. The more you do, the more objective you will be about every aspect of your money.

- **Review your financial position monthly.** Do this much like you would review your business' monthly financial statements.

- **Pay attention to trends.** If you have what looks like a continuing declining trend, stop, re-evaluate, and seriously consider changing your strategy. If you feel that requires firing your adviser, don't hesitate.

Appendix C

Terms and Conditions

This Publication is prepared strictly for the confidential use of our customer(s) and those advising our customers. This Publication is not intended for the direct or indirect solicitation of business. Weiss Ratings, Inc. expressly disclaims any warranty of merchantability or fitness for any particular purpose that may exist with respect to this Publication.

The information contained herein has been derived from data furnished by official sources that we deem reliable. However, Weiss Ratings, Inc. has not independently verified the data. The data and information contained herein are, therefore, provided "as is" without warranty of any kind. As such, Weiss Ratings, Inc. makes no warranty, express or implied, or representation as to the accuracy, adequacy or completeness of the information relied upon by it in preparing this Publication.

Weiss Ratings, Inc. uses the most current information in its possession during the rating review process. However, in the interim, company officials may have disclosed other information which could have a bearing on the opinions expressed in this Publication.

Weiss Ratings, Inc. disclaims any and all liability to any person or entity for any loss or damage caused, in whole or in part, by any error (negligent or otherwise) or other circumstances involved in, resulting from or relating to the procurement, compilation, analyses, interpretation, editing, transcribing, publishing and/or dissemination or transmittal of any information contained herein.

The ratings and other opinions contained in this Publication must be construed solely as statements of opinion from Weiss Ratings, Inc., and not statements of fact. Each rating or opinion must be weighed solely as a factor in your choice of a stock and should not be construed as a recommendation to buy, sell or otherwise act with respect to the particular product or company involved.

This Publication and the information contained herein is copyrighted by Weiss Ratings, Inc. Any copying, displaying, selling, distributing or otherwise delivering of this information or any part of this Publication to any other person, without the express written consent of Weiss Ratings, Inc. except by a reviewer or editor who may quote brief passages in connection with a review or a news story, is prohibited.

Important Warnings and Cautions

1. **A rating alone cannot tell the whole story.** Please read the explanatory information contained here. It is provided in order to paint a more complete picture of a common stock's strengths and weaknesses.

2. **Investment ratings shown in this book were intended for illustration.** The most recent ratings based on the most recent data are available in *The Ultimate Guided Tour of Stock Investing* at your local library, at www.WeissRatings.com, or by calling 1-800-289-9222.

3. **Stock prices change daily.** If a stock has experienced a significant price change since the date of our last evaluation, it could have a bearing on our opinion of the stock's prospects for the future. The ratings shown in this book were based on the stock prices as listed herein. Also, be aware that some stocks may have experienced a split since our evaluation, making share price comparisons difficult without further research.

4. **When deciding to buy or sell shares in a specific common stock, your decision must be based on a wide variety of factors in addition to the Weiss Investment Rating.** These include any charges you may incur from trading stocks, to what degree it meets your long-term planning needs, and what other choices are available to you.

5. **The Weiss Investment Ratings represent our opinion of a stock's risk-adjusted performance.** As such, a high rating means we feel that the common stock may perform well compared to other stocks. However, a high rating is not a guarantee that a stock will perform well, nor is a low rating a guarantee of weak performance. Many factors such as political events, legal actions, natural disasters, and other unforeseen occurrences can alter a stock's expected performance.

6. **A stock's individual performance is not the only factor in determining its rating.** Since the Weiss Investment Ratings incorporate performance relative to both the risk-free (Treasury) rate and market indexes, it is possible for a stock's rating to be upgraded or downgraded based strictly on the improvement or deterioration of these comparative factors.

7. **All stocks that have the same Weiss Investment Rating should be considered to be essentially equal from a risk/reward perspective.** This is true regardless of any differences in the underlying numbers which might appear to indicate greater strengths.

8. **Our rating standards are more consumer-oriented than those used by other rating agencies.** Other rating services often downplay investment risk and seldom if ever issue negative ratings. In fact, almost all brokerage firm opinions are either BUY or HOLD; sell recommendations are rare. The Weiss Investment Ratings are completely objective and exhibit a reasonable distribution of A, B, C, D, E and F rated stocks.

9. **We are an independent rating agency and do not depend on the cooperation of the companies whose common stocks we rate.** Our information is gathered from pricing and fundamental data obtained and documented on the open market. Although we seek to maintain an open line of communication with the companies' investor relations officers, we do not grant them the right to stop or influence publication of the ratings. This policy stems from the fact that this book is designed for the information of the consumer.

Appendix D

What Our Ratings Mean

A   **Excellent.** The company's stock has an excellent track record for providing strong performance with minimal risk, and it is trading at a price that represents good value relative to the company's earnings prospects. While past performance is just an indication – not a guarantee – we believe this stock is among the most likely to deliver superior performance relative to risk in the future. At the same time, "excellent" should not automatically be construed as a "buy" rating inasmuch as even the best stocks can decline in a down market.

B   **Good.** The company's stock has a good track record for delivering a balance of performance and risk. While the risk-adjusted performance of any stock is subject to change, we believe that this stock is a good value, with good prospects for outperforming the market. However, "good" should not automatically be construed as a "buy" rating since even good investments can decline in a down market.

C   **Fair.** In the trade-off between performance and risk, the prospects for the company's stock are about average based on its track record and current valuation. Thus, we feel it is neither a significantly better nor a significantly worse investment than most other common stocks. In short, there is no particular advantage to investing in this stock unless you believe that its future risk or reward profile will change.

D   **Weak.** The company's stock is an underperformer relative to other common stocks with a similar amount of risk. While the risk-adjusted performance of any common stock is subject to change, we believe that this stock represents a poor investment based on its current valuation and the company's current financial position. At the same time, "weak" should not automatically be construed as a "sell" signal since even weak stocks can rise in an up market.

E   **Very Weak.** The prospects for the company's stock are not good, with significant downside risks outweighing any upside potential. This opinion is based on the company's current financial condition in combination with the stock's historical risk-adjusted performance and current valuation. While the risk-adjusted performance of any stock is subject to change, we believe this stock is a poor investment risk. A "very weak" rating should not automatically be construed as a "sell" signal inasmuch as even bad investments can rise in an up market.

F   **Bankrupt.** The company issuing this stock is currently in bankruptcy proceedings. Typically, shareholders in a bankrupt company lose their entire investment when the company emerges from Chapter 11 reorganization or liquidates under Chapter 7. Therefore, we feel this stock has substantial downside risk for investors and very little, if any, upside potential.

+   **Plus sign** is an indication that the stock is at the upper end of the letter grade rating.

-   **Minus sign** is an indication that the stock is at the lower end of the letter grade rating.

U   **Unrated.** The stock is unrated for one or more of the following reasons: 1) It is too new to make a reliable assessment of its risk-adjusted performance. (Typically, a stock must have traded for at least one year before it is eligible to receive a Weiss Investment Rating.); 2) Quarterly reports filed with the SEC were either late or missing critical items that Weiss deems necessary for a thorough analysis; 3) Data anomalies exist that call into question either the accuracy or completeness of the information presently available to Weiss.

Appendix E

Table Column Definitions

Company Name

The name of the company that issued the common stock. If you cannot find the particular common stock you are interested in, or if you have any doubts regarding the precise company name, verify the information with your broker or on your account statement. Also, use the stock's ticker symbol for confirmation.

Industry Sector

The primary industry sector to which the company issuing the common stock belongs.

CD .... Consumer Discretionary
CS .... Consumer Staples
EN .... Energy
FN .... Financials
HC .... Health
IN .... Industrials
IT .... Information Technology
MA .... Materials
TS .... Telecommunications Services
UT .... Utilities

A blank stock type means that the stock has not yet been categorized.

Stock Ticker Symbol

The unique alphabetic symbol used for identifying and trading a specific common stock. No two stocks can have the same ticker symbol.

Overall Weiss Investment Rating

Our overall rating is measured on a scale from A to F based on each stock's risk-adjusted performance. This measure is a combination of the performance rating and risk rating assigned to a stock. The overall rating is not a simple average of the risk and performance grades. Rather it involves a dynamic assessment of how well investors have been compensated for the level of risk they have taken. See Appendix D for specific descriptions of each letter grade.

Stock Price

Closing price of a share of common stock on the date shown.

1-Year Total Return

The total return the stock has provided investors over the preceding twelve months. This total return figure is computed based on the stock's dividend distributions and share price appreciation/ depreciation during the period.

1-Year Total Return Percentile

The stock's percentile rank based on its one-year performance compared to that of all other common stocks in existence for at least one year. A score of 99 is the best possible, indicating that the stock outperformed 99% of the other common stocks. Zero is the worst possible percentile score.

3-Year Total Return

The total annual return the stock has provided investors over the preceding three years.

3-Year Total Return Percentile

The stock's percentile rank based on its three-year performance compared to that of all other common stocks in existence for at least three years. A score of 99 is the best possible, indicating that the stock outperformed 99% of the other common stocks. Zero is the worst possible percentile score.

Trailing Earnings Per Share

The company's net income from operations during the preceding 12 months divided by its number of outstanding common stock shares. This represents the amount of profit (loss) generated by the company for every share of outstanding stock.

Price-to-Earnings (P/E)
Also, known as the P/E ratio, this is the current stock price divided by the trailing annual earnings per share. A high P/E multiple indicates investors have high expectations for future growth and have bid up the stock's price in anticipation.

Dividend Rate
Dividend distributions provided to stock investors over the preceding 12 months.

Dividend Yield
Most recent quarterly dividend to stock investors annualized, expressed as a percent of the stock's current share price. Keep in mind that dividend income may be taxed at a different rate than capital gains depending on your income tax bracket.

1-Year Return Over Index Avg.
The total return the stock has provided investors over the preceding twelve months minus the total return over the preceding twelve months for their respective index. This is the excess return that an investor would have made being invested in the stock as opposed to the index.

Glossary

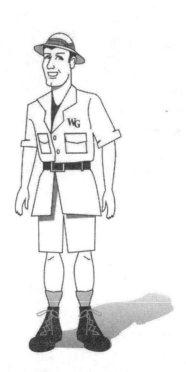

A Wise Glossary of Investing Terms

10-K – A formal version of a company's annual report, issued to the SEC.

10-Q – A formal version of a company's quarterly report, issued to the SEC.

401(k) Plan – A company-sponsored retirement savings plan that allows participants to make pre-tax contributions up to 15% of their annual salary or a maximum of $10,500 annually. These contributions grow tax-deferred until they are paid out, at which time the participant owes taxes on the amounts received.

52-Week High – Highest share price at which the stock has traded in the last 52 weeks.

52-Week Low – Lowest share price at which the stock has traded in the last 52 weeks.

3-Month Total Return – The total return the stock has provided investors over the preceding three months. This total return figure is computed based on the stock's dividend distributions and share price appreciation/ depreciation during the three month period.

6-Month Total Return – The total return the stock has provided investors over the preceding six months. This total return figure is computed based on the stock's dividend distributions and share price appreciation/ depreciation during the six month period.

1-Year Total Return – The total return the stock has provided investors over the preceding twelve months. This total return figure is computed based on the stock's dividend distributions and share price appreciation/ depreciation during the period.

1-Year Total Return Percentile – The stock's percentile rank based on its one-year performance compared to that of all other common stocks in existence for at least one year. A score of 99 is the best possible, indicating that the stock outperformed 99% of the other common stocks. Zero is the worst possible percentile score.

3-Year Total Return – The total annual return the stock has provided investors over the preceding three years.

3-Year Total Return Percentile – The stock's percentile rank based on its three-year performance compared to that of all other common stocks in existence for at least three years. A score of 99 is the best possible, indicating that the stock outperformed 99% of the other common stocks. Zero is the worst possible percentile score.

A

Accumulate – Broker/analyst recommendation that could mean slightly different things depending on the broker/ analyst. In general, it means to increase the number of shares of a particular security over the near term but not to liquidate other parts of the portfolio to buy a security that might skyrocket. A buy recommendation, but not an urgent buy.

Accumulated Deficit – The sum of losses resulting from a company's operations over time.

Acquisition of Assets – A merger or consolidation in which an acquirer purchases the selling firm's assets.

Acquisition of Stock – A merger or consolidation in which an acquirer purchases the seller's stock.

Adjusted Basis – Price from which to calculate and derive capital gains or losses upon sale of an asset. Account actions such as any stock splits that have occurred since the initial purchase must be accounted for.

Affiliate – A company that owns a significant, but non-controlling interest in the voting stock of another company.

Aggregate Debits – Customer-related receivables of the broker/dealer.

Aggregate Indebtedness – The debts of the brokerage firm that are not adequately secured or segregated according to the SEC's net capital and customer protection rules.

American Stock Exchange – The nation's second largest floor-based exchange, the American Stock Exchange ("Amex") has a significant presence in common stocks, index shares, and equity derivative securities. On the Amex, trading is conducted through an advanced centralized Specialist system combining the speed of computer-delivered orders with the liquidity of customer driven markets.

Analyst – Employee of a brokerage, investment advisory firm, or fund management house who studies companies and makes buy-and-sell recommendations on stocks of these companies. Most specialize in a specific industry.

Annual Report – Yearly record of a publicly held company's financial condition. It includes a description of the firm's operations, as well as balance sheet, income statement, and cash flow statement information. SEC rules require that it be distributed to all shareholders. A more detailed version is called a 10-K.

Arbitrage – Trading the same or similar security, commodity, or currency on two or more markets to take advantage of price differences.

Arbitration – Arbitration is a method where conflict between two or more parties is resolved by an impartial arbitrator who is knowledgeable in the area of controversy.

Ask – This is the quoted asking price, or the lowest price an investor will accept to sell a stock. Practically speaking, this is the quoted offer at which an investor can buy shares of stock; also called the offer price.

Asked – This is the lowest price at which anyone is willing to sell the security. If you are buying a security, you want to know its asked price. Stocks are usually quoted by "bid price" first, then "asked price."

Asset Allocation – The process of dividing a portfolio among major asset categories, such as bonds, stocks, or cash. The purpose of asset allocation is to reduce risk by diversifying the portfolio.

Averaging Down – Buying more of a security at a lower price than the original investment. The aim of averaging down is to reduce the average cost per unit of the investment.

B

Bear Market – Any market in which prices exhibit a declining trend for a prolonged period, usually falling by 20% or more.

Benchmark – A standard against which the performance of something (a stock) can be measured.

Bid – The highest price any buyer is willing to pay for a given security or commodity at a given time. In trading, we have the bid-ask-spread, which is the difference between what buyers are willing to pay and what sellers are asking for in terms of price. This is the highest price anyone is willing to pay to buy a security. If you are selling a security, you want to know its "bid price."

Blue-Chip Company – Used in the context of general equities, it is a large and creditworthy company, renowned for the quality and wide acceptance of its products or services, and for its ability to make money and pay dividends.

Bonds – A debt investment, with which the investor loans money to an entity (company or government) that borrows the funds for a defined period of time at a specified interest rate.

Book Value Per Share – The portion of the company's equity, or net worth, that is allocated to each share of stock.

Broker – An individual who is paid a commission for executing customer orders. Also, person who acts as an intermediary between a buyer and seller, usually charging a commission. A broker who specializes in stocks, bonds, commodities, or options acts as an agent and must be registered with the exchange where the securities are traded.

Broker/Dealer – Any SEC-registered firm that buys and sells securities, commodities, or other property for a commission. (See also "Investment Banker")

Brokerage Firm – When you buy or sell a security, you generally do so through a brokerage firm. Brokerage firms fall into two main camps: full-service brokers and discount brokers. Discount brokers charge far lower commissions than full-service brokers, and a growing number of deep discounters charge especially low commissions. But there is a trade-off. If you use a discount broker, you will get little or no investment advice, so you must be willing to make your own buy and sell decisions. A full-service broker, on the other hand, will help you pick investments and devise a financial plan.

Bull Market – Any market in which prices are in an upward trend.

Buy – To purchase an asset; also referred to as "taking a long position."

Buy Limit Order – A conditional trading order that indicates a security may be purchased only at the designated price or lower.

C

Call Option – An option contract that gives its holder the right (but not the obligation) to purchase a specified number of shares of the underlying stock at the given strike price, on or before the expiration date of the contract.

Capital – The net worth of a company, or the difference between its assets and its liabilities. The basic components of capital, or stockholder's equity, are common and preferred stock and retained earnings. (See also "Capitalization Index" and "Net Capital")

Capitalization Index – An index that measures the adequacy of the company's capital resources to deal with potentially adverse economic or market conditions that could arise. It is based on an evaluation of the firm's net capital, required net capital, and stockholders equity.

Cash and Equivalents – The value of assets that can be converted into cash immediately, as reported by a company. Usually includes bank accounts and marketable securities, such as government bonds and Banker's Acceptances. Cash equivalents on balance sheets include securities (e.g., notes) that mature within 90 days.

Cash & Securities Segregated – Customer cash accounts and fully-paid-for securities required to be segregated by the Customer Protection Rule. (See also "Customer Protection Rule")

Cash Dividend – A cash payment distributed to stockholders from the issuer. Dividends are distributed from current earnings and profits and are taxable income to the stockholder. Dividends can be held in your brokerage money market fund account or can be sent to you.

Chasing the Market – Purchasing a security at a higher price than expected because prices are rapidly climbing, or selling a security at a lower level when prices are quickly falling.

Churning – Excessive trading to generate commissions.

Close a Position – In the context of general equities, eliminate an investment from one's portfolio.

Commercial Paper – Short-term IOUs issued by corporations to meet short-term financing needs.

Common Stock – Securities that represent equity ownership in a company. Common shares let an investor vote on such matters as the election of directors. They also give the holder a share in a company's profits via dividend payments or the capital appreciation of the security.

Compounding – The ability of an asset to generate earnings that are then reinvested and generate their own earnings.

Consensus Forecast – The mean of all covering financial analysts' forecasts for a company.

Coverage Initiated – Usually refers to the fact that analysts begin following a particular security. This usually happens when there is enough trading in it to warrant attention by the investment community.

Critical Ranges – Guidelines developed to help you evaluate the levels of each index contributing to a company's Weiss Safety Rating. The sum or average of these grades does not necessarily have a one-to-one correspondence with the final rating for an institution because the rating is derived from a wider range of more complex calculations.

Current Ratio – The ratio of short-term assets to short-term liabilities, indicating the ease with which the firm can cover its short-term obligations in a period of adversity without having to liquidate its longer-term holdings. (See also "Liquidity")

CUSIP Number – A unique 9-digit identification number that identifies all stocks and registered bonds.

Customer Protection Rule – The rule issued by the Securities and Exchange Commission requiring that a broker physically segregate, from its own trading accounts, any cash or securities that have been fully paid for by the customer.

D

Day Order – An order to buy or sell securities today that automatically expires at the close of today's trading unless it is executed or canceled.

Debt to Equity Ratio or Debt Ratio – Total debt expressed as a percentage of total capital. (See also "Leverage")

Discount Broker – A brokerage firm that generally charges lower commissions than those charged by a full-service brokerage firm, but whose services are typically limited to executing buy and sell orders. (See also "Full-Service Broker" and "Online Broker")

Diversification – A risk management technique that mixes a wide variety of investments within a portfolio. It is designed to minimize the impact of any one security on overall portfolio performance.

Dividend – A portion of a company's profit paid to common and preferred stock holders. A stock selling for $20 a share with an annual dividend of $1 a share yields the investor 5%.

Dividend Reinvestment Plan (DRIP) – Automatic reinvestment of shareholder dividends in more shares of a company's stock, often without commissions. Some plans provide for the purchase of additional shares at a discount to market price. Dividend Reinvestment Plans allow shareholders to accumulate stock over the long term using dollar cost averaging. The company usually administers the DRIP without charges to the holder.

Dividend Per Share – The amount of the dividend that will be distributed to each outstanding share.

Dividend Yield – Most recent quarterly dividend to stock investors annualized, expressed as a percent of the stock's current share price. Keep in mind that dividend income may be taxed at a different rate than capital gains depending on your income tax bracket.

Dollar Cost Averaging – A method of investing. Money is invested at regular intervals in the same investment. Because you invest the same amount each time, you automatically buy less of the investment when its price is higher and more when its price is lower. Though the method doesn't guarantee a profit or guard against loss in declining markets, the average cost of each share is usually lower than if you buy at random times. For dollar cost averaging to work you must continue to invest regularly over time and purchase shares in both market ups and downs.

Dow Jones Index – The New York Stock Exchange (NYSE) index, which reflects the movement of the world's first stock market. It is composed of the 32 most traded stocks of the NYSE. Currently there are three more Dow Jones Indexes. The Dow Jones Industrial Average (DJIA) which is composed of 30 industrial stocks. The Dow Jones Transport Average (DJTA) composed of 20 stocks belonging to the transport industry (by rail, land or air) and finally DJUA (Dow Jones Utility Average), which is composed of 15 stocks belonging to the electrical and gas sectors.

Due Diligence – The process of checking the accuracy of information contained in a company public statement, such as a prospectus, before recommending that company to others. Is also the act of one company investigating another company before buying its shares.

E

Earnings Per Share (EPS) – A company's profit divided by its number of outstanding shares. If a company earning $2 million in one year had $2 million shares of stock outstanding, its EPS would be $1 per share. In calculating EPS, the company often uses a weighted average of shares outstanding over the reporting term.

Earnings Surprises – Positive or negative differences from the consensus forecast of earnings by institutions such as IBES, First Call or Zack's. Negative earnings surprises generally have a greater adverse effect on stock prices than a positive earnings surprise.

Employee Stock Ownership Plan (ESOP) – A program encouraging employees to purchase stock in their company.

F

Fail-To-Deliver – The failure by the broker representing the seller to deliver securities or commodities to the broker representing the buyer.

Fail-To-Receive – Notification by the broker representing the buyer that he has not received securities purchased from the broker representing the seller.

Fast Market – A term used to describe periods of rapid change within the various securities markets.

Financial Analysts – Also called securities analysts and investment analysts. Professionals who analyze financial markets, equities, and other financial vehicles, in order to write reports recommending either purchasing, selling, or holding various stocks.

Fiscal Year – Accounting period covering 12 consecutive months over which a company determines earnings and profits. The fiscal year serves as a period of reference for the company and does not necessarily correspond to the calendar year.

Forward Contract – A contract that obligates the buyer to purchase a given asset on a specific date at a price agreed to at the time of the contract. Unlike a futures contract, however, the value of a forward contract is settled at maturity. Also, forward contracts carry default (or credit) risk. (See also "Futures Contract.")

Full-Service Broker – A brokerage firm which typically provides a full range of services to its customers, such as trading, asset management, and financial advice including buy and sell recommendations. (See also "Discount Broker" and "Online Broker.")

Fundamental Analysis – Security analysis that seeks to detect misvalued securities through an analysis of the firm's business prospects. Research often focuses on earnings, dividend prospects, expectations for future interest rates, and risk evaluation of the firm.

Futures Contract – A contract that obligates the buyer to purchase a given asset on a specific date at a price agreed to at the time of the contract. Unlike a forward contract, however, the value of a futures contract is settled daily. Also, there is not default risk from the counterparty since participants must post a performance bond. Default risk from the exchange itself remains, however. (See also "Forward Contract.")

G

Good 'til Cancelled Order (GTC) – An order to buy or sell stock that is good until you execute or cancel it. Brokerages usually set a limit of 30-60 days, at which the GTC order expires if not restated.

Government Agency Securities – Securities issued by U.S. Government agencies such as the Government National Mortgage Association (GNMA or Ginnie Mae). These securities may or may not have the full faith and credit guarantee of the U.S. Government, depending on the issuing agency.

Government Securities – Any government-issued security, including Treasury securities, government agency securities, and government sponsored securities.

Government-Sponsored Securities – Securities issued by private corporations sponsored or supported by the U.S. Government such as the Federal National Mortgage Association (FNMA or Fannie Mae). Although these securities have an implied backing by the U.S. Government, such backing is not guaranteed.

Growth Stocks – Stocks that usually pay little or no dividend, instead, invests their earnings back into the company in hopes of fast growth.

H

Haircuts – Downward adjustments made to the assets held by a brokerage firm in accordance with the relative risk and volatility of those assets. Haircuts are used specifically for the purpose of determining a broker's net capital.

Hedging – Investment strategies used to offset the risk of a decline in the market value of securities, commodities, or other assets owned.

Hold – To maintain ownership of a security over a long period of time. "Hold" is also a recommendation of an analyst who is not positive enough on a stock to recommend a buy, but not negative enough on the stock to recommend a sell.

Holding Company – A corporation owning a controlling interest in a firm's voting stock.

I

Income Stocks – Stocks that pay high and regular dividends. (Less risky)

Index – Statistical composite that measures changes in the economy or in financial markets, often expressed in percentage changes from a base year or from the previous month. Indices measure the ups and downs of stock, bond, and some commodities markets, in terms of market prices and weighting of companies in the index.

Industry Sector – The primary industry sector to which the company issuing the common stock belongs.

Initial Public Offering (IPO) – A company's first sale of stock to the public. Securities offered in an IPO are often, but not always, those of young, small companies seeking outside equity capital and a public market for their stock. Investors purchasing stock in IPOs generally must be prepared to accept considerable risks for the possibility of large gains.

Insider Information – Material information about a company that has not yet been made public. It is illegal for holders of this information to make trades based on it, however received.

Insider Trading – Trading by officers, directors, major stockholders, or others who hold private inside information allowing them to benefit from buying or selling stock.

Insiders – Directors and senior officers of a corporation – in effect, those who have access to material, non-public information about a company. An insider also is someone who owns more than 10% of the voting shares of a company.

Investment Banker – A company that is involved in underwriting and selling new securities to the public.

Investment Strategy – A strategy, or plan of attack, an investor uses when deciding how to allocate capital among various investments including stocks, bonds, money markets, commodities, and real estate. The strategy should take into account the investor's tolerance for risk as well as future needs for capital.

Individual Retirement Account (IRA) – A retirement savings vehicle usually funded with pre-tax contributions that allows an investment to grow tax-deferred. (See also "Roth IRA")

J

January Effect – Refers to the historical pattern that stock prices rise in the first few days of January. Studies have suggested this holds only for small-capitalization stocks. In recent years, there is less evidence of a January effect.

Junk Bonds – Bonds of speculative or noninvestment grade, involving higher-than-average yield and risk. Specifically, these include all bonds with an S&P rating of BB or lower.

K

Keogh Plan – A retirement plan whereby a self-employed person may set aside a certain portion of income (tax deferred) into a retirement account. The money is taxable upon withdrawal at retirement when the person's tax bracket is often lower.

L

Legal Actions – This is the total of all regulatory actions, arbitrations, criminal actions, civil judicial actions, bonds, bankruptcies, judgments and liens recorded with the NASD.

Leverage – The degree to which an investor or business is utilizing borrowed money. For companies, leverage is measured by the debt-to-equity ratio, which is calculated by dividing long-term debt by shareholders' equity. The more long-term debt there is, the greater the financial leverage and the greater the risk of the company falling on its face.

Liabilities – Debts or creditors' claims against the company.

Limit Order – An order to buy or sell a security at a specific price or better. When you place a limit order to sell, provide your broker with a minimum sales price. When you place a limit order to buy, provide a maximum purchase price. Limit orders are day orders or GTC orders.

Liquidity – The degree to which a company can readily convert its assets into cash to meet current obligations.

M

Margin – The funds placed on deposit by a customer in order to borrow additional funds for the purchase of securities.

Margin Account – A brokerage account in which borrowed funds have been used, or are expected to be used, to finance the purchase of securities.

Marginal Tax Rate – The rate at which a person is taxed on each incremental dollar of income. In other words, the amount of income taxes owed on the last dollar earned.

Mark To Market – To adjust the value of a security to reflect its current market price.

Market Index – Market measure that consists of weighted values of the components that make up a certain list of companies. A stock market tracks the performance of certain stocks by weighting them according to their prices and the number of outstanding shares by a particular formula.

Market Order – Buying or selling securities at the price given at the time the order reached the market. A market order is to be executed immediately at the best available price and is the only order that guarantees execution.

Market Trading Times – U. S. stock markets are open for trades from 9:30 a.m. to 4:00 p.m. Eastern Standard Time.

Merger – Acquisition in which the buyer absorbs all assets and liabilities; or, more generally, any combination of two companies. The firm's activity in this respect is sometimes called M&A (merger and acquisition).

N

NASD (See "National Association of Securities Dealers")

National Association Of Securities Dealers – The nonprofit organization whose members include virtually all investment banking houses and firms dealing in the over-the-counter market. It is supervised by the SEC and its basic purposes are to: 1) standardize practices for securities trading, 2) establish high moral and ethical standards, 3) represent members in consultation with the government and investors, 4) establish and enforce rules, and 5) establish a disciplinary body to enforce the above provisions.

NASDAQ (See "National Association of Securities Dealers Automated Quotation System")

National Association of Securities Dealers Automated Quotation System – The computerized system owned and operated by the NASD which lists price quotations for securities traded over the counter and stocks traded on other exchanges.

Nasdaq Stock Market – The first electronic stock market listing over 5,000 companies. The Nasdaq stock market comprises two separate markets, namely the Nasdaq National Market, which trades large, active securities and the Nasdaq Smallcap Market that trades emerging growth companies.

Net Capital – The capital of the brokerage firm after adjusting total equity for the firm's illiquid assets and for the risk associated with its securities portfolio.

Net Capital Ratio – The ratio of net capital to total assets. This answers the question, how many cents of net capital does the firm have for every dollar of assets? The net capital ratio is the key ratio used by the SEC to track a firm's financial stability.

Net Capital Rule – The Securities and Exchange Commission rule requiring that brokers maintain enough capital and liquid assets to ensure the protection of their customers, creditors, and investors. (See also "Required Net Capital")

Net Profit – Gross sales minus taxes, interest, depreciation, and other expenses, also called net earnings or net income or bottom line.

New York Stock Exchange (NYSE) – A marketplace in which shares, options, and futures on stocks, bonds, commodities, and indices are traded. Also known as the Big Board or the Exchange. More than 2,000 common and preferred stocks are traded on the NYSE. Founded in 1792, it is the oldest exchange in the United States and the largest. It is located on Wall Street in New York City.

NYSE Composite Index – Composite index covering price movements of all new world common stocks listed on the New York Stock Exchange. It is based on the close of the market on December 31, 1965, at a level of 50.00 and is weighted according to the number of shares listed for each issue. Print changes in the index are converted to dollars and cents so as to provide a meaningful measure of changes in the average price of listed stocks. The composite index is supplemented by separate indices for four industry groups: industrial, transportation, utility, and finance.

Off-Balance Sheet Instruments – Financial instruments used to hedge the risk of assets and liabilities on the balance sheet of the broker/dealer. These instruments may also be bought and sold strictly for their profit potential. (See also "Off-Balance Sheet Risk")

Off-Balance Sheet Risk – The risk incurred by the use of highly complicated off-balance sheet financial instruments. This can be market and/or credit risk. (See also "Off-Balance Sheet Instruments.")

Online Broker – A brokerage firm that generally charges lower commissions than those charged by discount or full-service brokerage firms, but whose services are only available via the Internet. (See also "Discount Broker" and "Full-Service Broker.")

Option – Gives the buyer the right, but not the obligation, to buy or sell an asset at a set price on or before a given date. Investors, not companies, issue options. Buyers of call options bet that a stock will be worth more than the price set by the option (the strike price), plus the price they pay for the option itself. Buyers of put options bet that the stock's price will drop below the price set by the option. An option is part of a class of securities called derivatives, which means these securities derive their value from the worth of an underlying investment.

Options – Contracts granting the right to buy or sell securities or commodities at a specific price and within a limited time period.

OTC (See "Over The Counter")

Overall Weiss Investment Rating (See "Weiss Investment Rating")

Over The Counter – The securities market conducted through a telephone and a computerized network rather than the floor of a stock exchange. (See also "NASDAQ")

P

Payable To Broker/Dealers And Customers – Debts owed to other brokers and customers that arise out of securities transactions.

Portfolio – The group of assets—such as stocks, bonds and mutual funds—held by an investor.

Preferred Stock – Investors owning preferred stocks receive fixed dividend payments from the corporations, but they hold no voting rights on management issues. Preferred stocks are similar to bonds in that they do not normally participate in the rise or fall of the common stock.

Price Appreciation – When the share price of a stock increases in value.

Price to Projected EPS – Analyst forecasts used in the context of a P/E ratio based on forward (expected) earnings rather than on the trailing earnings.

Price-to-Book or P/B Ratio – Current stock price divided by common stockholder equity per share (i.e. book value).

Price-to-Earnings or PE Ratio – Current stock price divided by the trailing annual earnings per share. Assume XYZ Co. sells for $25.50 per share and has earned $2.55 per share this year; $25.50 divided by $2.55 equals 10. Therefore, XYZ stock sells for ten times earnings. Earnings per share for the P/E ratio are determined by dividing earnings for the past 12 months by the number of common shares outstanding. A higher P/E means investors have higher expectations for future growth and have bid up the stock's price.

Principal – The actual amount contributed into an investment, not including any monies earned from the investment itself.

Principal Transactions – Transactions in which the broker is buying or selling securities as a principal rather than as an intermediary. In principal transactions, the broker buys or sells for his own trading account and not for the customer's account.

Projected EPS – The earnings per share value that is expected in the future.

Put Option – An option contract giving the owner the right, but not the obligation, to sell a specified amount of an underlying security at a specified price within a specified time. The put option buyer hopes the price of the shares will drop by a specific date.

R

Rebalancing – The process in which an investor re-evaluates the weightings of each asset within the portfolio.

Receivables From Broker/Dealers And Customers – Assets due to a company from other brokers and customers.

Regulatory Actions – Regulatory actions initiated by the SEC, CFTC, other federal regulatory agencies, states, SROs, or foreign financial regulatory authorities that result in a finding of a violation and/or sanction or the issuance of an order. Also includes pending regulatory proceedings that could result in a regulatory action.

Repos – Short-term agreements to sell securities whereby the seller agrees to repurchase them at an agreed upon price and usually at a stated time. (See also "Reverse Repos")

Required Net Capital – The minimum net capital that a brokerage firm must maintain in accordance with SEC rules. (See also "Net Capital Rule")

Retained Earnings – Profits not paid out in dividends that are kept by a corporation to help finance expansion.

Return on Invested Capital – Income before extraordinary items during the preceding 12 months as a percentage of Total Invested Capital. Total Invested Capital includes outstanding issues of common stock, preferred stock, long-term debt, and minority interests.

Reverse Repos – Short-term agreements to purchase securities whereby the buyer agrees to resell them at an agreed upon price and usually at a stated time. (See also "Repos")

Reverse Stock Split – A proportionate decrease in the number of shares, but not the total value of shares of stock held by shareholders. Shareholders maintain the same percentage of equity as before the split. For example, a 1-for-3 split would result in stockholders owning one share for every three shares owned before the split. After the reverse split, the firm's share price is, in this example, three times the pre-reverse split price. A firm generally institutes a reverse split to boost its stock's market price to attract investors or avoid delisting due to low share price.

Right – An offer to existing stockholders of a company to purchase shares of a new issue of stock below public offering price.

Risk – The chance that an investment's actual return will be different than expected. This includes the possibility of losing some or all of the original investment.

Risk/Reward Trade Off – A balance that an investor must establish between the desire for low risk and the lure high returns. Low levels of uncertainty (low risk) are associated with low potential returns, whereas high levels of uncertainty (high risk) are associated with high potential returns.

Roth IRA – Introduced for the 1998 tax year, this type of IRA is funded with after-tax contributions, allowing the investor to withdraw tax-free principal and earnings at a later date.

S

S&P 500 Index – A barometer of the stock market based on the 500 largest publicly traded firms in terms of market capitalization. Since it is impractical for an individual investor to own such a large and diverse group of equities, some mutual funds attempt to mimic the stocks included in this index to achieve comparable performance.

Sales Per Share – The portion of the company's sales allocated to each share of stock.

Savings Bonds – U. S. government bonds issued by banks, savings and loans, and credit unions in denominations ranging from $50 to $10,000. These cannot be sold in a brokerage account.

SEC (See "Securities and Exchange Commission")

Secondary Market – The market for buying and selling existing securities, as opposed to buying new securities currently being issued by a corporation or a government body.

Sectors – A particular group of securities that are in the same industry.

Securities – Investment instruments reflecting either ownership in a company (stock), a creditor relationship (a bond), or a right to ownership (an option, right, or warrant).

Securities Act Of 1933 – The federal act covering many areas, including the new issues of securities, the regulation of disclosure, and anti-fraud provisions.

Securities Act Of 1934 – The federal act covering secondary market transactions. (See also "Secondary Market")

Securities And Exchange Commission – The federal regulatory agency created by the Securities Act of 1934 to administer that act along with the Securities Act of 1933. It is charged with promoting full public disclosure and protecting the public against malpractice in the securities markets.

Securities Borrowed – Stocks or bonds borrowed from customers and other brokers to facilitate transactions.

Securities Investor Protection Corporation – The nonprofit corporation that insures customer accounts of member firms against the failure of those firms. Accounts are insured up to $500,000 with a limit of $100,000 in cash.

Securities Loaned – Stocks or bonds loaned to customers and other brokers.

Securities Owned – Stocks and bonds held in a broker's portfolio primarily for principal transactions. (See also "Principal Transactions")

Securities Purchased Under Agreements To Resellm (See "Reverse Repos")

Securities Sold, Not Yet Purchased – Borrowed securities that are sold to profit from an expected price decline, also known as short positions or short sales.

Securities Sold Under Agreements to Repurchase (See "Repos")

Sell-Limit Order – Conditional trading order that indicates that a security may be sold at the designated price or higher.

Settlement Date – Stocks are currently traded with a "T+3" settlement date. For example, if Monday is the trade date, then the settlement date is Thursday. On the settlement day, cash or cleared securities must be in the account to avoid extension charges or possible penalties for canceling the trade.

Shareholder – Any person, company, or other institution that owns at least 1 share in a company. A shareholder may also be referred to as a stockholder.

Shares – Certificates representing ownership of stock in a corporation or company.

Short Positions (See "Securities Sold, Not Yet Purchased")

Short Sale – The act of selling a borrowed security that the investor does not own in the hopes of buying it back later at a lower price.

SIPC (See "Securities Investor Protection Corporation")

Spread – (1) Gap between bid and ask prices of a stock or other security. (2) Simultaneous purchase and sale of separate futures or options contracts for the same commodity for delivery in different months. Also known as a straddle. (3) Difference between the price at which an underwriter buys an issue from a firm and the price at which the underwriter sells it to the public. (4) Price an issuer pays above a benchmark fixed-income yield to borrow money.

Stock – A type of security that signifies ownership in a corporation and represents a claim on part of the corporation's assets and earnings.

Stock Exchanges – Formal organizations, approved and regulated by the Securities and Exchange Commission (SEC), that are made up of members who use the facilities to exchange certain common stocks. The two major national stock exchanges are the New York Stock Exchange (NYSE) and the American Stock Exchange (ASE or AMEX). Five regional stock exchanges include the Midwest, Pacific, Philadelphia, Boston, and Cincinnati. The Arizona Stock Exchange is an after-hours electronic marketplace where anonymous participants trade stocks via personal computers.

Stock Power – A stock power is a separate document from a stock or bond certificate. It is attached to a certificate when the certificate is deposited into a brokerage account. Acting as a power of attorney, the document transfers a registered security from the owner listed on the front of the security to another party (transfer agent or clearing firm). A person can sign the back of the registered security or they can use a stock power document.

Stock Price – Closing price of a share of common stock on the date shown.

Stock Split – A proportionate increase in the number of shares, but not the total value of shares of stock held by shareholders. Shareholders maintain the same percentage of equity as before the split. For example, a 2-for-1 split would result in stockholders owning two shares for every one share owned before the split. After the stock split, the firm's share price is, in this example, one-half the pre-split price.

Stock Ticker Symbol – The unique alphabetic symbol used for identifying and trading a specific common stock. No two stocks can have the same ticker symbol.

Stop-Limit Order – This is an order to buy or sell a security at a specified price or better, but only after a given stop price has been reached or passed.

Stop-Loss Order – An order to sell a stock when the price falls to a specified level.

Stop Order – An order to buy or sell becomes a market order once the market price reaches or passes the stated price. Stop prices are not guaranteed. A stop order to buy must be placed at a price higher than the current market price. One to sell must be placed at a price lower than the current market price. Note: A NASDAQ-listed stock cannot have a "stop loss" order placed on it.

Subordinated Liabilities – A debt whose holder has a secondary or junior claim to other general creditors.

Swap Contract – Obligates two parties to trade or "swap" specific cash flows at specific time periods. The interest rate swap, in which the cash flows are determined by two different interest rates, is the most common. The swap, like the futures contract, is settled at many settlement dates, but does not have the default risk protection of the performance bond. Therefore, it has less default risk than the forward contracts, but more risk than the futures contracts.

T

Tax-Deferred – The situation wherein the income and/or capital gains from an investment are not subject to income taxes in the year earned but may be subject to income taxes at a later date.

Tax-Free – The situation wherein no taxes are owed on the investment or its earnings.

Technical Analysis – Security analysis that seeks to detect and interpret patterns in charts depicting past security prices.

Ticker Symbol – (See "Stock Ticker Symbol")

Total Assets – The total of all assets listed on the company's balance sheet. This includes any of the company's resources having commercial or exchange value.

Total Invested Capital – A tally of all the outside investments a company's management has used to finance its business — everything from equity (the amount of stock sold) to long-term debt. It is calculated by taking the sum of common and preferred stock equity, long-term debt, deferred income taxes, investment credits and minority interest. Total invested capital is the denominator of the debt-to-total-capital ratio, a ratio that measures how leveraged a company is.

Total Market Capitalization – The total dollar value in millions of all outstanding shares of a company computed as shares outstanding times current market price. Market capitalization is a measure of overall corporate size.

Trade Date – The date when terms of the transaction, such as the price and quantity are established.

Trading Account – Securities owned by the brokerage firm itself. It consists of stocks and bonds in the broker's portfolio. (See also "Principal Transactions")

Treasury Securities – Securities issued by the U.S. Treasury that have the full faith and credit guarantee of the U.S. Government. These debt instruments are issued for the purpose of financing the federal deficit.

U

Underwriting – The business of purchasing securities from the issuing corporation for resale to the public. (See also "Investment Banker")

V

Volatility – A measure of risk based on the standard deviation of the asset return. Volatility is a variable that appears in option pricing formulas, where it denotes the volatility of the underlying asset return from now to the expiration of the option. There are volatility indices, such as a scale of 1-9; a higher rating means higher risk.

Voting Stock – The shares in a corporation that entitle the shareholder to vote.

Warrant – A contract which grants the holder the right to purchase a proportionate amount of common stock or bonds at a stated price (usually higher than market price at the time it is issued) for a certain period of time.

Weiss Investment Rating – Our overall rating is measured on a scale from A to F based on each stock's risk-adjusted performance. This measure is a combination of the performance rating and risk rating assigned to a stock. The overall rating is not a simple average of the risk and performance grades. Rather, it involves a dynamic assessment of how well investors have been compensated for the level of risk they have taken.

Weiss Performance Rating – A letter grade rating based on the common stock's performance and the company's growth prospects, as well as economic factors, without any consideration for the amount of risk the stock poses. Like the overall Weiss Investment Rating, the Performance Rating is measured on a scale from A to F for ease of interpretation.

Weiss Risk Rating – A letter grade rating based on the stock's risk as determined by its share price volatility and the company's financial stability, as well as economic factors. The risk rating does not take into consideration the overall financial performance the stock has achieved or the total return it has provided to its shareholders. Like the overall Weiss Investment Rating, the Risk Rating is measured on a scale from A to F for ease of interpretation.

Whisper Number – An unofficial earnings estimate of a company given to clients by a security analyst if there is more optimism or pessimism about earnings than shown in the published number. These are often found on the Internet.

Weiss Ratings Products

Ultimate Guided Tour of Stock Investing

This important new reference guide from Weiss Ratings is just what librarians around the country ordered — a step-by-step introduction to stock investing for the beginning to intermediate investor.

The easy-to-navigate guide explores the basics of stock investing and includes the intuitive Weiss Investment Rating on more than 6,000 stocks.

340 pages | Paperback | 8.5"x11" | $249 single | $499 quarterly

Top-Rated Stocks Service

Just when expert guidance is the most critical, investors are scratching their heads wondering who to trust. Weiss Ratings' **Top-Rated Stocks Service** tells the honest truth about the stocks that offer the BEST potential and the ones that are just too risky!

Weiss Ratings' top-rated stocks yielded 21.24% gains over the last 12 months, while the S&P 500 managed a measly 12.53%. Our monthly service culls out the top-rated stocks with absolutely no conflict-of-interest to muddy the waters. Knowing the top performers just got easier!

Single (1 issue) $69 | 1-Year (12 issues) Subscription $295

Weiss Ratings' Watchdog Service

Want to keep an eye on the rating of your bank, insurer, or investment? Weiss makes it easy with our Watchdog Service. You provide the name of the bank, insurer or investment you're interested in and our tracking service alerts you immediately if the Weiss Safety or Investment Rating changes, giving you timely advice regarding the implications of the upgrade or downgrade. Plus, each quarter you'll receive a new Consumer Safety Update reaffirming the current rating.

Paperback | 8.5"x11" | $48 annual service

Weiss Ratings' Consumer Guides provide the critical information you need to make sound financial decisions. Whether you're in the market for insurance or investments, each guide is packed with the accurate, unbiased information and recommendations you've come to expect from Weiss. We explain things so YOU can understand them without the aid of an MBA. Weiss Ratings' Consumer Guides help remove the guesswork and confusion with straight talk and sound guidance.

Consumer Guide to Homeowners Insurance

The **Consumer Guide to Homeowners Insurance**, a complete how-to guide, will help you understand homeowners insurance, select the appropriate type of insurance for your home, and ways to save money on your insurance premium.

82 pages | Paperback | 8.5"x11" | $49 single | $119 quarterly

Consumer Guide to Elder Care Choices

Planning for your golden years is more important today than it ever has been. To have peace of mind, it's crucial to find out about care options available including: Continuing Care Retirement Communities, Assisted Living Facilities, Home Health Care Agencies, Adult Day Care, and Nursing Homes.

50 pages | Paperback | 8.5"x11" | $49 single (annual edition)

Consumer Guide to Long-Term Care Insurance

The **Consumer Guide to Long-Term Care Insurance** helps you determine whether or not you, or a loved one, need long-term care insurance and if so, how to purchase the right policy.

72 pages | Paperback | 8.5"x11" | $49 single | $119 quarterly

Consumer Guide to Variable Annuities

Variable annuities are one of the fastest growing investment vehicles on the market today. But are they right for you?

The **Consumer Guide to Variable Annuities** leads you step-by-step to provide a thorough understanding of when variable annuities make sense and how they actually work.

42 pages | **Paperback** | **8.5"x11"** | **$49 single (annual edition)**

Consumer Guide to Auto Insurance

The **Consumer Guide to Auto Insurance**, an easy-to-use, how-to guide, will help you understand the auto insurance coverage required by your state, select the appropriate type of insurance for your vehicle, and ways to save money on your insurance premium.

80 pages | **Paperback** | **8.5"x11"** | **$49 single** | **$119 quarterly**

Consumer Guide to
Medicare Supplement Insurance

The **Consumer Guide to Medicare Supplement Insurance** leads you step-by-step on how to select a Medigap policy. Outlined are the 10 Standard Medigap Benefit Plans (A-J), along with the average premium rates based on age and gender. Also included is the Weiss Safety Rating on each company writing Medigap policies in the United States.

76 pages | **Paperback** | **8.5"x11"** | **$49 single** | **$119 quarterly**

Weiss Ratings' Shopper's Guides arm you with the <u>customized</u> information you need to make sound purchasing decisions. Each comes packed with information that is personalized to your unique situation. For example, when purchasing a long-term care insurance policy, age and location play a part in the pricing structure that companies use. Our Shopper's Guides provide you with the key elements, such as pricing, availability and types of services, so you can make the best decision!

Shopper's Guide to Long-Term Care Insurance

Each report is customized for you based on your age and state of residence, providing an apples-to-apples comparison of the long-term care insurance options available in your area, with price comparisons for long-term care insurance based on your age, gender, and location. Long-term care policies are grouped based on comparable benefit features, followed by a complete list of each policy's benefits.

Plus, you get the current Weiss Safety Rating for each company to help you identify the insurers that are most likely to be around when you need them.

Paperback | 8.5"x11" | $49 single customized edition

Shopper's Guide to Medicare Supplement Insurance

If you're a senior citizen, or care for one, our customized *Shopper's Guide to Medicare Supplement Insurance* is for you. In addition to providing a list of nearly all the insurers offering Medigap policies in your area, our report shows *price comparisons for each company* based on your age, gender, and location.

Paperback | 8.5"x11" | $49 single customized edition

Shopper's Guide to Term Life Insurance

Find price comparisons for term life insurance based on your age, gender, zip code and other unique information. You'll find the insurers who are currently offering the best rates.

Paperback | 8.5"x11" | $49 single customized edition

Individual Ratings Online

Now, you can easily keep up with our latest ratings through the Weiss Ratings website. This online summary covers any company's Weiss Safety Rating or an investment's unique Weiss Investment Rating. This convenient and inexpensive option gives you immediate access to ratings 24 hours-a-day for **stocks, banks and thrifts, HMOs, life insurers, mutual funds**, and **property insurers**.

**Online: http://www.weissratings.com/ratings_online.asp
$14.99 each**

Ratings Over the Phone

Weiss Ratings offers individual ratings over the telephone. Our knowledgeable customer service representatives will provide a company's Weiss Safety Rating or an investment's unique Weiss Investment Rating, along with a full description of what that rating means, for **stocks, banks and thrifts, HMOs, life insurers, mutual funds**, and **property insurers**.

Call 1-800-289-9222 | $19.00 each

2 Easy Ways to Order

Call our Customer Hotline at 1-800-289-9222

Order Online at www.WeissRatings.com

Weiss Ratings' Library Partnership

Weiss Ratings produces more in-depth reference versions of this book packed with information on the stocks you own, or are looking to buy. Our goal, with the help of your local library, is to make this information readily available to all consumers. If you're interested in learning more about any stock listed on the NYSE, Nasdaq or AMEX simply visit your local library's reference desk and ask for:

Weiss Ratings' Stock Guides

This reference guide contains reliable insight into the risk-adjusted performance of over 9,000 stocks. The Weiss Ratings' unique investment rating system makes it easy to see exactly which stocks are on the rise and which ones should be avoided. The following pages are samples taken from the ***Weiss Ratings' Ultimate Guided Tour of Stock Investing*** so you can see exactly what information is available at your local library.

Also at your local library is ***The Weiss Ratings' Guide to Common Stocks*** with both the Weiss Rating and the supporting analysis showing growth trends, profitability, debt levels, valuation levels, the top stocks in each industry, and much more.

Stock Ratings List Contents

1. Company Name.
The name of the company that issued the common stock. If you cannot find the particular common stock you are interested in, or if you have any doubts regarding the precise company name, verify the information with your broker or on your account statement. Also, use the stock's ticker symbol for confirmation. (See column 2.)

2. Stock Ticker Symbol
The unique alphabetic symbol used for identifying and trading a specific common stock. No two stocks can have the same ticker symbol.

3. Industry Sector
The primary industry sector to which the company issuing the common stock belongs.

CD	Consumer Discretionary
CS	Consumer Staples
EN	Energy
FN	Financials
HC	Health
IN	Industrials
IT	Information Technology
MA	Materials
TS	Telecommunications Services
UT	Utilities

A blank stock type means that the stock has not yet been categorized.

4. Exchange
The stock exchange that this stock trades on. A stock exchange is an organized marketplace in which stocks are traded by members acting as brokers for buyers and sellers of stock. Each exchange has requirements for membership so each stock only trades on one exchange. The largest exchanges — on which all but the smallest stocks trade — in the U.S. are the New York Stock Exchange, the American Stock Exchange, and the NASDAQ.

5. Market Index

The market index that this stock should be compared against. The market index is a measure that consists of weighted values of the components that make up a certain list of companies. A stock market index tracks the performance of certain stocks by weighting them according to their prices and the number of outstanding shares by a particular formula.

6. Overall Weiss Investment Rating

Our overall rating is measured on a scale from A to F based on each stock's risk-adjusted performance. Please see Appendix D for the description of each letter grade. Also, refer to the Forward for information on how our ratings are derived. Most important, when using this rating, please be sure to consider the warnings in Appendix C regarding the ratings' limitations and the underlying assumptions.

7. Weiss Performance Rating

A letter grade rating based on the common stock's performance and the company's growth prospects, as well as economic factors, without any consideration for the amount of risk the stock poses. Like the overall Weiss Investment Rating, the Performance Rating is measured on a scale from A to F for ease of interpretation.

8. Weiss Risk Rating

A letter grade rating based on the stock's risk as determined by its share price volatility and the company's financial stability, as well as economic factors. The risk rating does not take into consideration the overall financial performance the stock has achieved or the total return it has provided to its shareholders. Like the overall Weiss Investment Rating, the Risk Rating is measured on a scale from A to F for ease of interpretation.

Stock Ratings List

Company Name	Stock Ticker Symbol	Industry	Stock Exchange	Market Index(es)	Overall Weiss Investment Rating	Weiss Perform-ance Rating	Weiss Risk Rating
1-800 CONTACTS INC	CTAC	CD	NASDAQ	NASDAQ, R2000, W5000	D+	C-	D
1-800-FLOWERS.COM	FLWS	CD	NASDAQ	NASDAQ, R2000, W5000	C	B	C-
1MAGE SOFTWARE INC	ISOL	IT	NASDAQ	W5000	D	D	E+
1ST CONSTITUTION BANCORP	FCCY	FN	NASDAQ	NASDAQ, W5000	B	B+	C
1ST NET TECHNOLOGIES INC	FNTT	IT	NASDAQ	W5000	U	U	U
1ST SOURCE CORP	SRCE	FN	NASDAQ	NASDAQ, R2000, W5000	B-	B	C+
1ST ST BANCORP INC	FSBC	FN	NASDAQ	NASDAQ, W5000	B-	B	C+
21ST CENTURY HOLDING CO	TCHC	FN	NASDAQ	NASDAQ, W5000	B	A-	C
21ST CENTURY HOLDING CO	TCHCW	FN	NASDAQ	W5000	U	U	U
21ST CENTURY INS GROUP	TW	FN	NYSE	R2000, W5000	C+	B-	C+
21ST CENTURY TECHNOLOGIES	TFCT	CD	NASDAQ	W5000	C-	C+	D-
24/7 REAL MEDIA INC	TFSM	IT	NASDAQ	NASDAQ, R2000, W5000	C	C+	D
360NETWORKS INC	TSIXQ	TS	OTC	W5000	U	U	U
3CI COMPLETE COMPLIANCE CORP	TCCC	IN	NASDAQ	W5000	C-	C+	D-
3COM CORP	COMS	IT	NASDAQ	NASDAQ, W5000	D+	C-	D
3D SYSTEMS CORP	TDSC	IN	NASDAQ	NASDAQ, W5000	C-	C	D+
3DFX INTERACTIVE INC	TDFXQ	NA	OTC	W5000	U	U	U
3DO CO	THDOQ	IT	OTC	W5000	U	U	U
3M CO	MMM	IN	NYSE	DOW, SP500, W5000	A+	A+	B
3SI HOLDINGS INC	TSIH	IT	NASDAQ	W5000	U	U	U
4 KIDS ENTERTAINMENT INC	KDE	CD	NYSE	R2000, W5000	B-	B+	C-
4-D NEUROIMAGING	FDNU	HC	OTC	W5000	U	U	U
4NET SOFTWARE INC	FNSI	IT	NASDAQ	W5000	C-	C	D-
7-ELEVEN INC	SE	CS	NYSE	W5000	C	A+	C-
724 SOLUTIONS INC	SVNX	IT	NASDAQ	NASDAQ, W5000	D-	E	D
800 TRAVEL SYSTEMS INC	IFLYQ	CD	NASDAQ	W5000	U	U	U
8X8 INC	EGHT	IT	NASDAQ	NASDAQ, W5000	D-	E+	E+
99 CENTS ONLY STORES	NDN	CD	NYSE	R2000, W5000	C	C+	D

A

Company Name	Stock Ticker Symbol	Industry	Stock Exchange	Market Index(es)	Overall Weiss Investment Rating	Weiss Perform-ance Rating	Weiss Risk Rating
A B WATLEY GROUP INC	ABWG	FN	OTC	W5000	U	U	U
A CONSULTING TEAM INC	TACX	IT	NASDAQ	NASDAQ, W5000	C	B	D-
A D A M INC	ADAM	HC	NASDAQ	NASDAQ, W5000	C-	B	D-
A NOVO BROADBAND INC	ANVB	IN	OTC	W5000	U	U	U
A S V INC	ASVI	IN	NASDAQ	NASDAQ, R2000, W5000	B	B+	C
A.C. MOORE ARTS & CRAFTS INC	ACMR	CD	NASDAQ	NASDAQ, R2000, W5000	B-	B+	C-
AAIPHARMA INC	AAIIE	HC	NASDAQ	W5000	D	D	E+
AAMES FINANCIAL CORP.	AMSF	FN	NASDAQ	W5000	C	B+	E+
AAMPRO GROUP INC	AAPO	IN	NASDAQ	W5000	U	U	U
AAON INC	AAON	IN	NASDAQ	NASDAQ, R2000, W5000	B	B	B
AAR CORP	AIR	IN	NYSE	R2000, W5000	C-	C	D
AARON RENTS INC	RNT	CD	NYSE	R2000, W5000	A+	A+	B+
AARON RENTS INC	RNT.A	CD	NYSE	W5000	A+	A+	B+
AASTROM BIOSCIENCES INC	ASTM	HC	NASDAQ	NASDAQ, W5000	D-	E+	D-
AAVID THERMAL TECHNOLOGIES	AATT	IT	OTC	W5000	U	U	U
ABATIX CORP	ABIX	IN	NASDAQ	NASDAQ, W5000	C-	C	D
ABAXIS INC	ABAX	HC	NASDAQ	NASDAQ, R2000, W5000	B+	A	C+
ABB LTD -ADR	ABB	IN	NYSE	W5000	D+	C	D
ABBEY NATIONAL PLC	ABYNY	FN	NYSE	W5000	U	U	U
ABBEY NATIONAL PLC -ADR	ANB.PA	FN	NYSE	W5000	U	U	U

Market Indices Listed: Russell 2000, Wilshire 5000, Dow Jones Industrial Average, S&P 500, and Nasdaq Composite Index
Industry/Sector Codes: CD=Consumer Discretionary; **CS**=Consumer Staples; **EN**=Energy; **FN**=Financials; **HC**=Health; **IN**=Industrials;
IT=Information Technology; **MA**=Materials; **TS**=Telecommunication Services; **UT**=Utilities

Company Name	Stock Ticker Symbol	Industry	Stock Exchange	Market Index(es)	Overall Weiss Investment Rating	Weiss Perform- ance Rating	Weiss Risk Rating
ABBOTT LABORATORIES	ABT	HC	NYSE	SP500, W5000	B-	A-	C-
ABC BANCORP	ABCB	FN	NASDAQ	NASDAQ, R2000, W5000	B-	A	C-
ABER DIAMOND CORP	ABER	MA	NASDAQ	NASDAQ, W5000	C+	B-	D
ABERCROMBIE & FITCH -CL A	ANF	CD	NYSE	W5000	B	A-	C-
ABGENIX INC	ABGX	HC	NASDAQ	NASDAQ, R2000, W5000	D	D+	D
ABIGAIL ADAMS NATL BANCORP	AANB	FN	NASDAQ	NASDAQ, W5000	B-	B+	C
ABIOMED INC	ABMD	HC	NASDAQ	NASDAQ, R2000, W5000	D+	C	D
ABITIBI CONSOLIDATED INC	ABY	MA	NYSE	W5000	D+	C-	D
ABLE ENERGY INC	ABLE	EN	NASDAQ	NASDAQ, W5000	C-	C+	D-
ABLE LABORATORIES INC	ABRX	HC	NASDAQ	NASDAQ, R2000, W5000	B-	B	C
ABLEAUCTIONS.COM INC	AAC	IN	AMEX	W5000	D	D+	D-
ABLEST INC	AIH	IN	AMEX	W5000	C	C+	C
ABM INDUSTRIES INC	ABM	IN	NYSE	R2000, W5000	B+	B+	B
ABN AMRO HOLDING NV -ADR	ABN	FN	NYSE	W5000	U	U	U
ABOVENET INC	MFNXQ	TS	OTC	W5000	U	U	U
ABOVENET INC	ABVT	TS	OTC	W5000	U	U	U
ABRAMS INDUSTRIES INC	ABRI	IN	NASDAQ	NASDAQ, W5000	D+	C	D
ABRAXAS PETROLEUM CORP/NV	ABP	EN	AMEX	W5000	D+	C+	E+
ABSA GROUP LTD -ADR	ABSXY	FN	OTC	W5000	U	U	U
ABSOLUTE WASTE SVCS INC	ABWS	MA	OTC	W5000	U	U	U
ABSS CORP	ABSP	NA	NASDAQ	W5000	U	U	U
ABX AIR INC	ABXA	IN	NASDAQ	W5000	U	U	U
ACACIA RESEARCH- COMBIMATRIX	CBMX	HC	NASDAQ	NASDAQ, W5000	D	E+	D
ACACIA RESEARCH-ACACIA TECH	ACTG	IT	NASDAQ	NASDAQ, W5000	D+	C	D-
ACADIA REALTY TRUST	AKR	FN	NYSE	R2000, W5000	C+	B	C-
ACAMBIS PLC -ADR	ACAM	HC	NASDAQ	NASDAQ, W5000	U	U	U
ACCELR8 TECHNOLOGY CORP	AXK	IT	AMEX	W5000	C-	C	D
ACCELRYS INC	ACCL	IT	NASDAQ	NASDAQ, R2000, W5000	U	U	U
ACCENTURE LTD	ACN	IT	NYSE	W5000	B	B	B
ACCEPTANCE INSURANCE COS	AICI	FN	OTC	W5000	U	U	U
ACCERIS COMMUNICATIONS INC	ACRS	TS	NASDAQ	W5000	U	U	U
ACCESS ANYTIME BANCORP INC.	AABC	FN	NASDAQ	NASDAQ, W5000	C+	B+	D+
ACCESS INTEGRATED TECH	AIX	IT	AMEX	W5000	U	U	U
ACCESS PHARMACEUTICALS INC	AKC	HC	AMEX	W5000	D-	E+	E+
ACCESS WORLDWIDE CMMNCTNS	AWWC	CD	NASDAQ	W5000	C-	B-	E+
ACCESSITY CORP	ACTY	HC	NASDAQ	NASDAQ, W5000	D	D	D
ACCESSPOINT CORP.	ASAP	IT	OTC	W5000	U	U	U
ACCIDENT PREVENTION PLUS	ACPL	CD	NASDAQ	W5000	U	U	U
ACCLAIM ENMNT INC	AKLM	IT	NASDAQ	NASDAQ, W5000	U	U	U
ACCREDITED HOME LENDERS	LEND	FN	NASDAQ	NASDAQ, R2000, W5000	C-	B	E+
ACCREDO HEALTH INC.	ACDO	HC	NASDAQ	NASDAQ, W5000	B	A-	C
ACCRUE SOFTWARE INC.	ACRUQ	IT	OTC	W5000	U	U	U
ACCUFACTS PRE-EMPLOYMENT	APES	IN	NASDAQ	W5000	C	A-	D+
ACCUPOLL HOLDING CORP	ACUP	IT	NASDAQ	W5000	E+	E+	E+
ACE CASH EXPRESS INC	AACE	FN	NASDAQ	NASDAQ, R2000, W5000	B	A-	B-
ACE COMM CORP	ACEC	IT	NASDAQ	NASDAQ, W5000	D	E+	D-
ACE LIMITED	ACE	FN	NYSE	SP500, W5000	B	A-	B-
ACETO CORP	ACET	IN	NASDAQ	NASDAQ, R2000, W5000	A+	A+	B-
ACI TELECENTRICS INC	ACIT	CD	OTC	W5000	U	U	U
ACLARA BIOSCIENCES INC	ACLA	HC	NASDAQ	NASDAQ, W5000	C-	C-	D

Market Indices Listed: Russell 2000, Wilshire 5000, Dow Jones Industrial Average, S&P 500, and Nasdaq Composite Index
Industry/Sector Codes: **CD**=Consumer Discretionary; **CS**=Consumer Staples; **EN**=Energy; **FN**=Financials; **HC**=Health; **IN**=Industrials;
IT=Information Technology; **MA**=Materials; **TS**=Telecommunication Services; **UT**=Utilities

Company Name	Stock Ticker Symbol	Industry	Stock Exchange	Market Index(es)	Overall Weiss Investment Rating	Weiss Performance Rating	Weiss Risk Rating
ACMAT CORP	ACMT	IN	NASDAQ	W5000	C	B	D+
ACMAT CORP -CL A	ACMTA	IN	NASDAQ	NASDAQ, W5000	C+	B+	C-
ACME COMMUNICATIONS INC	ACME	CD	NASDAQ	NASDAQ, W5000	D	D	D
ACME METALS INC	AMIIQ	MA	OTC	W5000	U	U	U
ACME UNITED CORP	ACU	CD	AMEX	W5000	B+	A	B-
ACNB CORP	ACNB	FN	NASDAQ	W5000	C	A-	D
ACORN HOLDING CORP	AVCC	IT	OTC	W5000	U	U	U
ACR GROUP INC	ACRG	CD	NASDAQ	W5000	C	A-	C
ACS-TECH80 LTD	ACSEF	IT	NASDAQ	NASDAQ, W5000	B-	B+	C-
ACT MANUFACTURING INC	ACTMQ	IT	OTC	W5000	U	U	U
ACT TELECONFERENCING INC	ACTT	CD	NASDAQ	NASDAQ, W5000	D+	C-	D-
ACTEL CORP	ACTL	IT	NASDAQ	NASDAQ, R2000, W5000	C	C	C-
ACTERNA CORP	ACTRQ	IT	NASDAQ	W5000	U	U	U
ACTION PERFORMANCE COS INC	ATN	CD	NYSE	R2000, W5000	C	C+	D
ACTION PRODUCTS INTL INC	APII	CD	NASDAQ	NASDAQ, W5000	D+	C-	D-
ACTIONVIEW INTERNATIONAL INC	AVWI	CD	NASDAQ	W5000	U	U	U
ACTIVCARD CORP	ACTIF	IT	NASDAQ	W5000	U	U	U
ACTIVCARD CORP	ACTI	IT	NASDAQ	NASDAQ, R2000, W5000	D+	C-	U
ACTIVCARD CORP	ACTIY	IT	NASDAQ	W5000	U	U	U
ACTIVE LINK COMMUNICATIONS	ACVE	IT	OTC	W5000	U	U	U
ACTIVE POWER INC	ACPW	IN	NASDAQ	NASDAQ, W5000	D	D	E+
ACTIVEWORLDS CORP	AWLD	IT	NASDAQ	W5000	U	U	U
ACTIVEWORLDS CORP	AWLDW	IT	NASDAQ	W5000	U	U	U
ACTIVISION INC	ATVI	IT	NASDAQ	NASDAQ, W5000	B-	B	C
ACTRADE FINL TECHNOLGIES LTD	ACRTQ	FN	OTC	W5000	U	U	U
ACTUANT CORP -CL A	ATU	IN	NYSE	R2000, W5000	B	B+	C+
ACTUATE CORP	ACTU	IT	NASDAQ	NASDAQ, R2000, W5000	C-	C	D
ACUITY BRANDS INC	AYI	IN	NYSE	R2000, W5000	B	A-	B
ACUSPHERE INC	ACUS	HC	NASDAQ	NASDAQ, W5000	U	U	U
ACXIOM CORP	ACXM	IT	NASDAQ	NASDAQ, W5000	B+	B+	B-
ADA-ES INC	ADES	MA	NASDAQ	W5000	U	U	U
ADAMS GOLF INC	ADGO	CD	NASDAQ	W5000	C	B+	D
ADAMS RESOURCES & ENERGY	AE	EN	AMEX	W5000	B	A-	C
ADAPTEC INC.	ADPT	IT	NASDAQ	NASDAQ, R2000, W5000	C	B-	D+
ADB SYSTEMS INTL LTD	ADBY	CD	NASDAQ	W5000	E+	E	E+
ADC TELECOMMUNICATIONS INC	ADCT	IT	NASDAQ	SP500, NASDAQ, W5000	D+	D+	D
ADDVANTAGE TECHNOLOGIES GP	AEY	IN	AMEX	W5000	B	A	C-
ADE CORP/MA	ADEX	IT	NASDAQ	NASDAQ, R2000, W5000	C+	B	D
ADECCO SA -ADR	ADO	IN	NYSE	W5000	U	U	U
ADELPHIA COMMUN -CL A	ADELQ	CD	NASDAQ	W5000	U	U	U
ADEPT TECHNOLOGY INC	ADTK	IT	NASDAQ	W5000	E+	E+	E+
ADESA INC	KAR	CD	NYSE	W5000	U	U	U
ADM TRONICS UNLIMITED INC/DE	ADMT	MA	NASDAQ	W5000	D	D+	D-
ADMINISTAFF INC	ASF	IN	NYSE	R2000, W5000	C+	B	D
ADOBE SYSTEMS INC.	ADBE	IT	NASDAQ	SP500, NASDAQ, W5000	B	A-	C
ADOLOR CORP	ADLR	HC	NASDAQ	NASDAQ, R2000, W5000	D	D-	D
ADRIAN RESOURCES LTD.	ADRRF	MA	NASDAQ	W5000	U	U	U
ADSERO CORP	ADSO	IN	NASDAQ	W5000	U	U	U
ADSTAR INC	ADSTW	IT	NASDAQ	W5000	U	U	U
ADSTAR INC	ADST	IT	NASDAQ	NASDAQ, W5000	D	E+	D-

Market Indices Listed: Russell 2000, Wilshire 5000, Dow Jones Industrial Average. S&P 500, and Nasdaq Composite Index
Industry/Sector Codes: CD=Consumer Discretionary; **CS**=Consumer Staples; **EN**=Energy; **FN**=Financials; **HC**=Health; **IN**=Industrials; **IT**=Information Technology; **MA**=Materials; **TS**=Telecommunication Services; **UT**=Utilities